AND THE WALLS
COME CRUMBLING
DOWN

AND THE WALLS COME CRUMBLING DOWN

TANIA DE ROZARIO

First published 2016 by Math Paper Press by BooksActually, Singapore
First North American edition 2020 by Gaudy Boy

A project supported by the Creation Grant

NATIONAL ARTS COUNCIL
SINGAPORE

Published by Gaudy Boy LLC,
an imprint of Singapore Unbound
www.singaporeunbound.org/gaudyboy
New York

For more information on ordering books, contact
jkoh@singaporeunbound.org.

ISBN 978-0-9994514-0-3

Cover design by Flora Chan
Interior design by Jennifer Houle

For the families we build from scratch.

CONTENTS

PREFACE

IT'S MAY 2020, and I'm sitting in my Vancouver apartment in the midst of a pandemic. Shops, schools, bars, libraries, museums—they're all closed. I've haven't touched anyone I know in over a month, or seen anyone I know outside the confines of a computer screen. I leave the building once a week for essentials, but because I have bad lungs, even that has become a series of strategies that involve masks, pocket-sized sanitiser, caution. Everything that enters my house upon return—groceries, packages, mail, my own body—is assumed to be contaminated and put through various rituals of cleaning or isolation. Yet even with all these measures, my front door, the fortress between inside and outside, has never felt so permeable. The virus does not require a key or a passcode to find its way into my home. All it needs is for me to forget my own vulnerability for just a second. To scratch an itch on my nose without washing my hands. To bump into a friend who walks her dog down my street and succumb, absentminded, to a hug.

Home (as a concept, not a building) has always been an uncomfortable abstraction for me. When I was 12 years old, a "lesbian exorcism" forced me to come to terms with the fact that my mother was never going to accept a queer daughter. My childhood flat stopped feeling like home around that time. In my teens, I learned that as a queer woman, my country was never going to accept me either. I eventually left my mother's apartment without telling her I was not coming back, and returned only 15 years later, when I heard she had died. I eventually left Singapore as well.

In my mid-20s, a romantic relationship I'd made the mistake of pouring all my feelings of home into, fell apart. We'd been living together for a number of years before she left the country, and a year after, me. For the first time, I found myself processing the fact that I was living alone in a country whose housing culture is hostile to anyone not living with their biological families, not straight-married, not rich. Despite all the love and support I received from close friends (and believe me, I thank my lucky stars for them), I still felt terribly alone. As per the country's cultural norms, all my friends my age were living with their parents, in their childhood homes, and would continue to do so until marriage. No friends my age had spent their 20s expending energy house-hopping from questionable rental to questionable rental on their own dime. I had no access to other queer people who were estranged from their families and realised that I was on the outside of what was considered a "normal" life. In this one breakup, I grieved a mother who did not love me, a girl who was leaving me, housing that seemed to keep spitting me out, and a country that saw me as deviant.

This book came out of that grieving.

I am so grateful at the moment to be safely housed. Even so, this pandemic has forced me to confront ideas of home in new ways. My choice to ride out my study permit and remain a settler in Vancouver over the course of this pandemic, even when Singapore was urging overseas students to come home, remains an uncomfortable one. When I started writing this book, I started somewhere in the middle, with the chapter titled "Walls". It was 2008, and I was in a long-distance relationship I did not realise was about to end, processing an argument we'd had over Skype. Over 10 years later, I'm writing this preface, and am again in a long-distance relationship, this time trying not to entertain worries about my partner getting sick while we are continents apart. I worry every day about her, as well as about what has become a huge extended chosen family of artists, queers, and activists. But I know that had I returned to Singapore, I would be worrying every day about my ability to return to Vancouver should the pandemic outlast my study permit and current immigration policies.

What happens when unbelonging is the space you are in but belonging is the people within that space? Being pulled in various directions this way so often feels like limbo, like moving forward in time but always being trapped in it.

In this book, time is also imperfect, non-linear. "Amorphous", if you are in a generous mood. "Disjointed", perhaps, if you are not. I wanted chapters to be linked thematically rather than chronologically, to reflect the process from which it emerged. "Walls," "Roof," and "Drawers" were written as stand-alone pieces in 2008/2009, long before I thought of them as being part of a single manuscript. Subsequent content emerged slowly over the next few years, as scenes or fragments. It was only when I decided to curate chapters in relation to housing that I fully realised the concept of the book. When this happened, I wrote the book's first chapter, followed by its final lines. Every other in-between came in fragments.

Even now, with this story far behind me, time still finds ways to remind me that our emotional lives are not truly linear. My ex and I have moved on, found paths to our respective happinesses, and remain friends to this day. And yet, there are still songs I used to listen to on flights between Singapore and Amsterdam that I cannot listen to on planes. When I do, I cry almost immediately. It's a physical, reflexive response that has nothing to do with her, but everything to do with this period of grief that somehow attached itself to spaces, objects, and inaccessible parts of myself trapped in time.

The nature of time in the book has had a huge impact on how people receive it as well. Even though the chapters were deliberately arranged in what I felt was an emotional arc, I've been told that the lack of linear chronology has suggested that they are single essays or prose-poems, rather than a single piece of work. I'm fine with this. I understand that there is a need for publishers and critics to know what shelf the book will sit on in stores, what subgenres are trending, which books are eligible for what prizes. Categorisation belongs to industry and not to art, and squeezing things to fit single genres is not my concern. Stories, like homes and time and grief, can't be fully contained: they spill out from under doors, slip out through cracks in the concrete, seep out through vents.

And on the unruliness of stories, and the impossibility of genre to contain them, I would like to end on this note: Many scenes in this book were written from personal memory, the most unreliable of archives—first-hand encounters reframed by time, perspective, and human fallibility. A number of scenes were created as fictional vignettes based on research—made-up stories inspired by essays and articles. Nothing in this book is hard fact. Nothing in this book is pure fantasy. For many, this begs the question of how it should be received.

One of my favourite authors, Cyril Wong, once said that when he writes, what he is doing is looking for people like him. I think that that is true for me too. A lot of people who've read this story—particularly young women and young queer-folk from Singapore—have told me that the book speaks to them. When I hear this, I don't necessarily think that I've written a great book, but that I've found people like me. I hope that in doing so, I've let someone else know that we share certain truths. I would like to think that in writing this, I've turned into the person I needed when I was younger—the young queer who felt outside of home.

I hope that by the time you receive this book, the pandemic keeping us apart will have come under control.

I hope that by the time you read this story, you feel safe enough to come inside.

AND THE WALLS
COME CRUMBLING
DOWN

HOLES IN THE WALL

EXPEL

THE NIGHT YOU called, the termites came. Hungry, wet from the rain.

They must have known the heart of the house had been emptied, must have decided to hollow out the roof while they still had time. After all, someone new might move in once I ran out of rent to pay. And this someone might demolish the buffet, tearing down the structure and cementing the walls, sealing up all the cracks in the floor that had granted them access to my life in the first place.

It felt as if one night was all it took to turn the roof protecting my head into the very thing that I was in danger of.

My house was falling apart. That is what the exterminator would tell me the next day. When I asked him to tell me something I didn't already know, he smiled smugly and told me I had three options: I could either deoxygenate my property (for a hefty sum of ten grand), poison the soil in my garden (inevitably killing all my plants), or spot-dust the structural wood with arsenic (inevitably killing me).

Seeing that I did not have ten grand, that I quite liked my plants, and that I did not regard the idea of death as particularly uninviting at the time, I opted for the arsenic.

It was only when you put down the phone that I heard them. That tiny, insistent sound. That crackle-and-pop that resembled a cross between television buzz and garlic being

1

fried. I had just walked back into my house when you hung up on me. You were staying at your parents' again and I was pissed. When I was finally confronted with silence and then a dial tone, I followed what sounded like static coming from my own head, into what had been our bedroom. Into what was now *my* bedroom.

The termites had built miniature tunnels all down one wall. Soil and faeces like veiny fingers trailed down from the roof, the tunnels providing adequate moisture and shelter for them to conduct their chewing.

I'd never seen termites before and I called you back in a panic. Your phone was off and I was outnumbered. Without anyone to share in this nightmarish lullaby of ten thousand unwanted guests chewing with their mouths open.

On clear nights when the sky is quiet, I think about the night we went in search of Mars. The papers had said it was the one time in three hundred years that it would be as bright as the moon and twice as big. We walked around the car park, holding hands, excited at the prospect of discovering, for us, what would be as good as a new planet.

We never found it. It was cloudy and it was 3am. A group of drunk teenagers, a few years younger than us, noticed our interlocked fingers and whispered. They looked up at the sky, trying to figure out what we were searching for. I smiled to myself. We had a secret. Planets to discover and so many nights ahead.

The romance was short-lived. The night ended in fighting the minute we got back. I can't even remember what started it. One of those arguments so inane that both parties become embarrassed that it even happened. Usually, it revolves around where things are supposed to go. Or around habits that annoy you for no logical reason. It's never the subject matter that makes you want to pull your hair out, but the constant repetition; incidents cloned one on top of the other, marking days like numbers crossed out on a calendar.

Back in bed, I was curled up like a fist. I could feel you contemplating behind me. You placed your hand on my hip. I ignored it. You kissed the back of my neck. I faltered. You apologised. I turned around and kissed you. And as the kisses got longer, warmer, harder, I placed my hands between your legs and found you wet.

Everything about you leads to home. Veins visible like tributaries running up your forearm. Skin mapping scars, creases, bends. And beyond the armour of your teeth, visceral constellations.

I remember thinking that we would probably never get to see Mars at all. Seeing that we had missed it that night. I wondered about all the things we might never get to do while we were together, as you climbed on top of me and became my universe.

———

Morning. I sit on my bed and watch termites scurry back into their trails. They are sound-sensitive. Once they sense vibrations, they return to their tunnels. One night on the internet, deprived of both lover and sleep, and I'm officially the resident termite expert. They're falling off the parapet because they are blind. Once fallen, they're goners; without their tunnels, their bodies dry out.

The trouble is, for the hundreds of bodies I've swept up, I know that there are a hundred thousand below the ground.

It's unfair really, the mathematics of it all.

Meanwhile, I've placed the feet of our bed in containers of oil. I've sealed all our paintings in gladwrap. I've put our clothes in polystyrene boxes and I've dabbed the doorframes with vetiver. I'm surrounded by so much synthetic material that everywhere I turn, something squeaks; I am starting to feel like a cartoon character. I roll my chair over the cracked portions of my floor, now lined with bubble wrap. My life is going downhill in a series of mini-explosions: Pop. Pop. Pop.

Never underestimate two things: The ability to romanticise despair into a story, and if that fails, the ability to retain one's sense of humour. If something can't be made into a book, it can surely be made into pretty amusing dinner conversation. Surely my house and heart falling to pieces is fodder for . . . *something*.

PACK

IT'S RAINY SEASON by the time I've booked my flight and the weather is seeping into every aspect of my life. Above and around the house, it pours. Plastic groundsheets line the floor and plastic buckets catch drips from my leaky ceiling. Nothing seems to hold water these days and I feel as though I, too, am leaking. This is the fourth house since leaving my mother's flat. Occupied for less than a month and already it is purging me out.

We thought this had been the one. But then again, for eight hundred dollars, any house would have been the one. You and I shared two rooms—one to sleep in and one to work in. We sublet the rest of the house to other artists who used the third room and the kitchen as workspaces. It was the ideal home. A place everybody could afford, in which beautiful things were created every day.

The space had not been occupied for years, and sat along a small lane in the Upper Thomson area. Prior to us, a construction company had stored its materials behind the bolted doors. Rumours of sex work still drew migrant workers to our doors, looking for leisure. By the time we were done with the place, it probably drew more attention to itself than it had before. One housemate painted the exterior façade red while the wall that separated us from the household on our left was covered in blackboard paint. The chalk drawings that changed

7

depending on whatever was happening that day, both amused and scared our neighbours. Our drawings of cartoon termites drinking champagne disturbed the exterminator, in particular.

Making the house livable had been a task that was almost surgical; opening up the very belly of its being in order to carve out a space that we could inhabit. Scrubbing out grime from between the tiles, evening out the walls so that they could be repainted, squeezing filler into gaps in the floor. There were some stains that could not be removed and we had no idea what had left them. We left those questions unasked as we employed every tool known (and unknown) to housekeeping to scrub, sterilise, unearth, re-fill, and fix. Hiring industrial experts to chemical clean the entire exterior cropped up in discussion and was forgotten after we found out how much that would cost.

There were some things, of course, that we could not resolve: the way the ceiling boards in the kitchen sloped downward a little too far, as though the shoulders of the house were permanently slumped; the fact that the kitchen was bereft of oven, stovetop, cabinets, food, *anything*; the fact that while the charm of this house was rooted in retro tiles which had not been changed for years and fittings that had not seen modification since the 60s, from this same charm snaked the open drain that still ran through the kitchen, dividing it from the living room. But then again, the drain had an upside: Unable to afford a washing machine, we hand-washed all our clothes, and it allowed us the convenience of squeeze-drying them above the metal gratings.

What we soon came to realise was that, despite the lack of furnishing and fittings, the house was not altogether unoccupied. Located near the reservoir and in close proximity with unprecedented amounts of greenery, the space had provided sanctuary to all sorts of creatures who would have otherwise remained wild; a Singapore I had never known, buried under the weight of time and concrete. A snail lived permanently on the wall of our bathroom, and centipedes came spasming out from between the tiles every time one of us showered. Bloated, black, furry caterpillars inched their way across the ceiling and fat roaches came in search of food that was never there. Spiders straight out of nightmares and as large as dinner plates slunk their ways into the kitchen to take shelter from storms.

Rainy days were the worst, with all of us seeking refuge under the same shelter.

Today, the plants are pleased about the downpour. They push themselves out of the soil in the backyard and insist their way up towards the sun that they know will reemerge. Out front, the downpour pockmarks chalk-drawn caricatures of us, soon to be washed away completely.

I'm sitting in my boxer shorts and a singlet that has not been washed in days. My hair is in some sort of similar crisis, matted enough to be concerning but not oily enough to warrant panic. There is no one else here. There has not been anyone else here for days. You are gone. Our housemates have not come in since the termite episode the week before. I seem to be the only person with nowhere to run to.

In the corner of the room, lizards click their tongues and come out of hiding. They know that the rain is driving termites out from the ground and into the roof, through the tunnels they created in the vertical beams. It's a feast for them tonight. I, on the other hand, am down to the last apple I stole from a petrol kiosk, where slanted mirrors were kind enough to let me slip out of the store like light.

I have a few friends who could lend me money but I've just paid off all debts, and I don't want more. I've friends who would cook me a meal. But I have irrational fears of asking for help.

Besides, I have a cheque clearing the next day and am not particularly hungry. Tomorrow I will be a wealthy woman, until the next person rich enough to commission words or images decides to pay me late.

The termites though, are having their fill. From the clicking sounds barely audible under the rain, the lizards are doing the same. I shudder, thinking about the spiders that might, in turn, be eyeing the lizards hungrily. I consider calling up the cable company and asking how I ended up living in one of their nature channels when I don't even have a television set.

I wish I had a cigarette.

This processing of payment is a waiting game that eats at your insides, makes you antsy. I try to remain as still as possible. Less energy expended means less hunger to feed. I cannot be bothered to unpack anything just to give myself something to do, so I resign myself to staring at the wall. My eyes end up moving to a black-and-white drawing—one of the things you left behind. Me, without clothes, arms above my head, staring straight back at myself, a charcoal mirror. Evidence that remaining still is no mean feat for me. That is, after all, how we met.

Taking my clothes off for money had not been the natural career choice. But it paid for art materials and was less cringe-worthy than ghostwriting ghost stories for local publishing houses. I had done the latter for a year while I was in school. It was easy work. But at two cents per word, there is only so much one person can say about long-haired women in white dresses lurking in wait for cabbies; or about army boys waking to the sight of headless ghouls.

The drawing instructor had said to do something with a twist. What artists call opposing curves. A figure throwing its weight to one side in a visual demonstration of gravity. I was told that I could look in any direction I wanted.

I turned to look at you.

It was, of course, premeditated. I had posed for your class the week before and could not get you out of my head, even though we had not spoken a word to each other. I was restless and infatuated, and you looked like a treat. I blabbed about you to my best friend every day for seven days. I had a lot to say about someone whose name I did not even know.

After the class was over, we exchanged smiles and I went to the toilet to scrub charcoal dust off the soles of my feet. I found them doing some sort of funny dance when I moved to leave. I shook it off and headed towards the exit, trying to scratch the itch out from under my eyelids. The image you had left behind was making the view of anything else intolerable. The plants lining the corridors annoyed me. The gate at the exit looked ridiculous. I was clearly walking in the wrong direction. I turned around and walked back to the drawing room.

I asked your name. You told me. My life hovered on the edge of a syllable. My mouth had found its purpose.

You came over to my work studio the week after. I'd asked you to model for some photographs. It was the perfect, if not overused, ploy. I shot 15 rolls of film over three months; a slow and expensive courtship for a fresh graduate. But there could have been no other way. You had a girlfriend. And I did not want a messy situation. Honesty was important. And so long as the camera stood between us, we were honest.

Three months later, we slept together. You had told me that the two of you had broken up. You had lied.

I lit a cigarette once we were done. I could not find my matches and used a candle lighter instead. You would tell me later that it was at that moment that you fell in love.

The rest happened like lightning: There you were in black-and-white, sitting and smiling in front of my lens. There you were, T-shirt and jeans, beside me in the wood workshop. There you were with a box of cereal, bringing breakfast to my studio. There you were asleep beside me, staying over because you'd missed your bus.

There you were, 3:00 a.m., me waking to find your eyes on me. There you were, in the morning, shirt riding up the flat of your stomach. There you were, hand in mine, lips on mine, skin against mine, limbs knotted with mine. And there you were, the next morning, and the next, and the next, and the next.

And there you were, in our kitchen, bringing the udon to a boil. There you were, curled into yourself, hair askew, covered in blanket and sleep. There you were, in my paintings, in my words, in my bed, in my arms, under my skin, inside my head, tripping accidentally into parts of myself I had no idea existed. And now here you are, leaving me at the airport. There you are in another country. There you are in a place I cannot find you, in a room I have no access to, on streets I do not recognise, whose names I cannot pronounce. I feel as though I am screaming while you take your leave in decrescendo.

What made us think it would last? What else could possibly happen to lovers apart for too long? All those gaps in between that could not be filled because neither of us had money for the constant commute. We saw each other for a month, twice a year. The body cannot deal with such extreme joy and despair; the inevitability of brokenness.

> *"I need to find someone else while I am here."*
> *"I didn't need to hear that."*
> *"I'm sorry."*
> *"Don't be. I'll be happy for you."*
> *"Yeah, right."*
> *"Well, the better half of me will be happy for you."*
> *"And the other half?"*
> *"The other half wants you to miss me always."*
> *"The better half of me will."*

Platitudes are poor substitutes for emotions, this negative space hollowed out and without words. I know the shape of you and it has no name. I know the sound of you and the smell of you and the touch and sight and taste of you. But language departed the same day you did, leaving my mouth empty.

The articulation of you is the articulation of me. I am the hole you left behind.

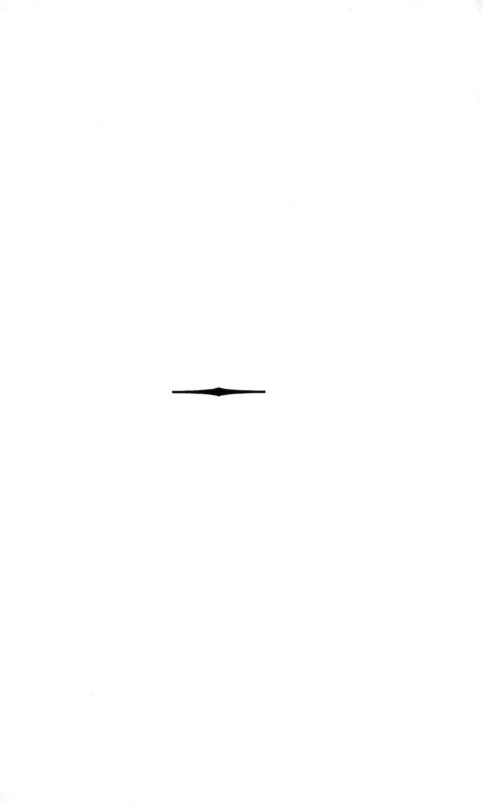

VACATE

I AM SLEEPING through turbulence.

I know because when I open my eyes, the flight attendant is wearing a look of alarm. I know because she actually has her hand on my shoulder and is shaking me. I wake with a start just as the plane dips, pushing my stomach up into my throat.

"Ma'am. Can you fasten your seatbelt?"

Her pleading expression disorientates me. Flight attendants are supposed to look reassuring and she looks about as reassuring as a thief with a smile. I look down at my lap, up at the lit seatbelt sign, and then to my left at the woman next to me who looks equally disconcerted.

"Are we . . ." My words are slurred. I wipe sleep from my mouth while struggling with the seatbelt. ". . . are we in some sort of trouble?"

"Weather's a little rougher than usual, that's all." She turns and looks at me. "I cannot believe you were sleeping."

The plane takes another dip and passengers let out a collective yelp of surprise. The woman next to me starts to laugh unsettlingly.

Not remembering where I am when I wake up has become routine. I lose track of the number of beds I've been in during the past few years. I've spent the last fortnight at a friend's house, sleeping in her study, because the sound of termites chewing at my walls had started giving me nightmares. I look again at the woman on my left, at the attendants buckling up their own seats, at the plastic cup from the water I'd drunk while ascending, stuffed into the seat pocket in front of me. I concretise my surroundings by naming every object I see. It's a grounding technique I learned over many years, dealing with self-harm: *Chair.* Pause. *Booklet.* Pause. *Tray table.* Pause. *Plane.* Pause. *Crash.* Ah, crap. So much for that.

I switch on the TV screen and check the flight tracker to find that we are two thousand miles to our destination. This is the seventh flight I've taken between Singapore and Amsterdam.

Fast forward.

When we meet at the airport this one last time, we will not bound towards each other with joy. We will not smile shyly at each other, embarrassed by our own enthusiasm. You will not ask me which midnight snack I picked on the plane.

This time, there will be knots in both our chests. One of them will be from wondering how to act around each other. Another because this anxiety should have never have been part of our vocabulary. Not us, lovers at first sight. Not us, best friends. Not us, not us, not us.

But that is what we are at this point: *Not us.*

We will embrace, saying nothing. You will turn away from me when I use the word *love.* I will tell you I've missed you terribly and you will take my laptop case, not touching my hair the way you used to, not running your fingers across my face the way you usually would, not cracking some silly joke that would make the months in between fall to the ground like tired children.

No. This time, our meeting will be all about the *nots*. Except when we are at the train station where you will tell me about how you slept with her. You will bike home from there and I will board the tram. I will call my best friend, hear her distant hello and cry, howling so loud that even the Dutch with their stoic, morning faces will peer at me with concern.

Fast forward.

We are having dinner at a squat kitchen with friends from Germany. Lentil soup, salad, two types of rice, banana chocolate truffle cake. Five euros. All vegan. She is standing on a crate and dishing out the soup. Midway through the main course, she comes to sit with us.

I'm on a break, she says, occupying the open spot to your left. You sit in between us. You don't look up. She is extremely refined. The polar opposite of me. She moves her food around neatly on her plate, her legs neatly crossed, each spoonful traveling neatly to her mouth. Her words are well-formed. Her face is well-formed. Her curls are well-formed. Everything that comes out of her mouth sounds so well put together, I am looking to see if there is a string in her back. Perhaps if I pull it, she will stick to *hello*.

Rewind.

We fight the minute we return from the airport. We fight while I lug my suitcase down the basement stairs. We fight when I start unpacking. We dance flames around each other till you clench fists, frustrated, yelling that it is *only sex*. You're *alone* here. You are *lonely*. Then the real rant begins.

You yell about being *unable to take her seriously*. After all, how can you? She's so *sanitised*, you're *afraid to get her dirty*. She's a shop full of crystal and you're driving a tractor. She's *polite and proper*. Good morning. Good night. Good evening. Good day. Good God, she's even proper in bed. You tell her you need it a little more rough. You tell her the names you like to be called. You tell her too: *It's just sex, it's just sex.* That deep, dark thing you need out of your system; that animal that needs to be broken.

I know how to break you. But this intensity confined to the quarters of our bed is no longer enough. When faced with the heat of lust, you reciprocate with fervour. But when faced with the price of love, you cower beneath the sheets. Love is too big for you. Too wide to straddle, too messy to control.

When I ask if you like it, you grow plump with desire, lips moist, face contorted with want.

When I ask if you'll fight for me, you shrink away, voice like a desert, doors closing one by one like shutters behind your eyes.

When she comes to sit with us, I resist the childish desire to crack a joke, to catch her off-guard. But it occurs to me then that she is the person I was six years before. She is ignorant of her role in this drama and I am not sure she even knows who I am. Realising that your lies are something she and I have in common, makes me swallow my words before they emerge. She seems so small compared to my rage, and compared to this affinity I now feel. Besides, she does not look like she's prepared to fight. At least not with anyone except herself.

Like me, she has scars running up both arms.

Rewind.

But that is yet to come. In this undefined space where we will fly circles around each other. In this unchartered territory where we will kiss so tenderly that our insides feel as though they might spill out of our mouths. Where we will hold each other so tightly that we will forget whose limbs are whose.

I hear a beep and realise the seatbelt sign has finally gone off. A nervous voice emerges from the cockpit, explaining the problems with the weather. It says that it is going to be smooth sailing the rest of the way.

FLY

THIS HOUSE IS a ghost of itself. Furniture sealed in plastic, everything an imprint of its former self. I run my fingers over the edges of chairs, over the bed frame, night table. It all feels the same: mummified. Everything packed like an artifact, this museum of us.

Here is the bed we bought the day we were finally able to afford it, nights of insomnia woven into the sheets. Here is the shape of your body compressed into tired springs as the mover uses up the last of the saran wrap on the mattress.

And then, all that is small enough, distilled into boxes, mouths taped shut.

When you first left for Europe, packing had been a matter of separating your necessities from mine. We thought this was an easy task, given that between us, we did not own very many things. We soon learned though, that the effects of having very little money could be very similar to having too much: every thing you owned became more precious than it actually was. Scraggly brushes, yellowing notebooks, packets of instant noodles. Everything you owned, still owned you. Even if it had come in a pack of five and cost two dollars.

I came home to find the studio overturned. Paintings backed furniture for support. Brushes and books discussed their future over minimal legroom and empty cartons. Packing, you wore rolls of tape like bangles.

I have secured an apartment. But I am so physically and emotionally tired from packing, I think I might like to seal *myself* into a cardboard box and label it *Used*. The sound of termites gets louder as the house gets emptier and as it turns slowly, like a simple change of set, into an empty space.

This is the room we no longer share. This is the bed, expanding to twice its size. These are the walls that will no longer eavesdrop on arguments, apologies, laughter, sex. This is the house emptying itself of us. This is the silence that will grow pregnant with days, packed one unspoken word after another.

———

When I was young, my grandfather used to position bowls of water underneath the dining room light, to catch flying ants that would fly into the light and fall. I started doing the same when I learned that flying termites could be dealt with in the same way. The winged breeders of both species emerge from the ground during the warm wet months, heading for the nearest source of light. I started setting up little water-traps all over the house. *Here you go, suckers*, I thought. *Smart enough to destroy a man-made structure, but stupid enough to drown in a glass of water.*

I often forget, when dealing with pests, that it is we who built our homes on top of theirs. In the wild, when termites emerge from their mounds, they encounter vast plots of empty land. The moon is their only source of light, a lighthouse that bears a single instruction: *Follow me.*

When the ground is moist and the evenings warm, the termites launch to the sky by the thousands, huge shadows swarming towards a goal never to be reached. They do it because they are programmed to. There is no intellectual reasoning or emotional conviction behind it. Flying towards the moon means flying the longest distance they can before shedding their wings like clockwork and falling to the ground to mate. It ensures that colonies are spread over a vast area. They do this because this is what they are.

And termites aren't the only creatures with an innately programmed sense of travel. The wild rock pigeon is said to have an inbuilt map and compass. Able to find its way home from two kilometres out, its instinctive homing mechanism is not programmed to locate general areas or the nearest light source, but the exact spot of its own nest, even from miles away. The bird will return to its original mate and will do so even through rain, heat, sandstorm. Its purpose is precise and it is bound to its home by a biology that distance cannot break.

After years of speculation, it was discovered that the pigeon's ability to find its way home—even if set free from a place devastatingly far and completely foreign—was connected to its ability to use sound waves to navigate; sound waves so low that they emanate from the very belly of the earth, rising up from oceans, moving through crusts and cut loose into the atmosphere.

How remarkable this ability, not yet detected in any other species. How tempting the thought of explaining it through human experience. The idea of having that one place that you not only can, but must return to. The idea that every flight out is just an inevitable recoil back; a token journey into the wild that lasts only as long as the earth allows.

Until the ocean speaks in a frequency only your heart can hear: Come home, come home.

———————

One of the last things I pack is an old photo of you. I find it in an old album you'd brought with you from your parents' place. Pigtails, kindergarten uniform, the little girl your parents always wanted but that you never grew up to be. It reminds me of a story you once told.

You were seven years old. Sun bright the way it only is when we are kids. You had wandered off alone. The way many children do and smart adults still try to. You enjoyed climbing trees, picking up rocks, catching grasshoppers with which you'd scare the other girls in the class.

You found the nest, nestled on a lower branch. Straw, sand, saliva. Not the perfect circle seen in children's books, but identifiable anyway. Mother Bird was nowhere in sight. Teacher was nowhere in sight. Classmates were nowhere in sight.

And then you saw the eggs.

When you told me the story, your face crumpled. Eyebrows furrowed, head tilted to the side. You scratched at the insides of your palms and your voice changed. It's amazing how the most vivid childhood memories often revolve around guilt and lessons we wish we'd learned second-hand. Your face pinched by regret and the bird that never was, never became, never got a chance.

When I think of birds' eggs, I cannot help but think of Winterson and how she described stealing another's heart, the way she would a bird's egg. Such an apt analogy on so many levels. That's how you stole mine, after all. Sleight of hand, a simple gesture. An unthinking action whilst I was not looking and then suddenly, the nest was empty.

What happened to us, lover? I flew through the sky to see you. Home was where you were. Where we were together. Not this space where we cling desperately to each other and yet tiptoe across eggshells as if they were mines.

You were seven years old. You slipped the egg into your pocket. Palm-sized home of a creature yet to exist. The object before life. Before birth. Prehistory in a shell. Broken before you even got back to class.

Perhaps you thought you'd see it hatch. Like in those videos back in school. Baby birds pecking their way out of crumbling wombs. First the tiny tapping. Then the hairline cracks. Then the almost elastic membrane beneath slowly stretching to puncture-point. And then, a beak.

But amidst the shells in which we used to nest, we break upon each other. And I am liquid in your palm, splinters in your pocket.

TEAR DOWN THE HOUSE

WINDOWS

IT WAS DARK down in the basement, even in the day. In Amsterdam, where light is already scarce during winter. We were living in what was supposed to be a storeroom. It was the polar opposite of my mother's flat, elevated 25 storeys aboveground. The only source of natural light was the little ventilation window that opened out into an equally small porch where people hung their laundry. The small luxury of seeing out often meant looking at people's feet as they took their clothes in from the rain.

Because we were underground, snails would sometimes make their way into the room. And once, when I was not there, a frog. How bizarre for any creature that might have been hopping along to find itself in the basement of some house, tangled amidst canvas, second-hand furniture, and leather boots. Thankfully, nothing ever found its way into the bed.

Except the lies.

The first time it happened, we were sitting on the steps of the university. It was an exceptionally sunny day and a hundred other people had come out into the afternoon sun to drink wine. In the Netherlands, the sun is a highly priced commodity, and people emerge when it does. The Dutch like order but the sun is cause for a break in routine. Walk through the city and you will see people perched on the ledges of their windows, taking in heat, faces drenched in daylight.

You told me you would be seeing some friends. I asked if you'd be seeing her. You got annoyed. You told me if that was what you wanted to do, you'd have told me so. You squinted at me and turned away. I could not tell whether it was because you were angry with me, or whether it was because the light was in your eyes. Either way, I knew you were lying.

The word *window* can be traced back to the word *eagpyrl*, which means *eye-door*, and later, *vindauga*, which some interpret as *the eye, open to the wind*.

So prized were windows that governments imposed a tax on anyone who had more than ten in their home. Views were a luxury and windows became a symbol of a person's wealth. Smarter citizens, of course, knew that what was being taxed was their access to light and ventilation. Some believe that this is where the phrase *daylight robbery* comes from.

In many cities, windows remain objects of contention. French architect Le Corbusier, whose visions of modernity would soon be reflected throughout cities like Singapore, scandalised the world with windows that ran horizontally instead of vertically. In Hong Kong, housing can still be valued or devalued based on window space. We underestimate how much of our culture revolves around windows and the illusion of freedom they provide. *Room with a view, window of opportunity, when God closes a door.*

Perhaps you and I should have made some sort of rule to never argue in that basement. To not fight where there was no light. To not surrender to those dark corners that seemed to swallow us whole each time we descended down those narrow stairs into the darkened hearts of ourselves.

The lie got bigger as the day passed, expanding like some strange balloon animal out of control. It mutated, grew limbs, sprouted strange appendages, got so large that it blocked your eyes out.

Or maybe that was just the dark that slipped itself in between our skins like eels. No embrace was tight enough to squeeze the truth from you; no kiss soft enough to coax it from your throat.

Before leaving in the morning, you picked a clean pair of trousers. Took an extra long time in the shower. Got annoyed when I asked if I could tag along for the errands, and left as swiftly as you lied. I was sitting at the corner of the bed. It was cloudy outside and we were saving on power. The only light besides that which came from the murky hole in the wall, dripped from the edges of your computer screen. I was supposed to look for directions to the cinema we were going to later that evening. Your email tab was open. Light from its window beckoned.

I looked at the door. I heard you go up the stairs, feeling the same way I did years ago when I stole money from my mother's wallet, buried beneath birth certificates and paperwork. It was during the few minutes she was gone, brushing her teeth. It was a betrayal of trust I felt no guilt over because my mother was someone for whom I felt nothing.

But you. You.

I clicked on the tab. Went to your Inbox. And then your Outbox.

Proof. I had it. It was liberating. Freeing. Made me want to scream and cry and break things. I was not crazy. I was not imagining things. You were a liar.

But now, so was I.

I closed the window and waited.

———

Scientists spent years balking at the idea that the eye was anything else but an organ able to detect light. Human personality could not be articulated through the eyes nor could human behaviour be estimated through them. A mockery of science at best. Poetic hogwash at worst. Sorry, all you poets who waxed lyrical across pages about all you saw in your lovers' eyes. Sorry all you lyricists who found a hundred ways to rhyme *eyes* at the end of chorus lines. The eye was just like any other part of our body. Functional.

Of course, science, as it so often does, started biting its own tongue when scientists in Sweden discovered that patterns in the iris were able to indicate particular personality traits. Apparently, there are correlations between eye structure and personality because the same genes responsible for the iris are also partially responsible for the frontal lobe of our brains.

Some of the alleged personality traits that can be detected from examining the iris include empathy, the ability to trust, impulsiveness, and a propensity to give in to cravings.

———————

I was leaving in two days. I could have closed that window when I had finished with your mail. Could have shut that tab, shut my mouth, shut my eyes, hopped on that plane and returned to my familiar life.

But I didn't. I left it open for you to find. An eye into your eye. A pound of flesh for another. I knew what you knew. I wanted you to know that I knew.

Is there something you want to tell me?

You started firing questions at me, getting increasingly upset with my refusal to respond. I shrugged, indignant. Surely you could not deny it, turning me into the very thing I hated. I'd made a choice I could not unmake. Had you been honest, we would not have been having this conversation at all.

I walked away from you without a word, and started packing. I dumped my clothes into the suitcase and zipped it up. I was leaving the next day, and this hell would end.

You ask me again. I say nothing. This time, you start to cry.

I feel myself grow numb. My body is saying it's either shutdown or breakdown.

I am a wall. I am a wall. I am a wall. I am a giant and I tower above you. I am a giant and I can't hear your voice. There is familiarity in this. I spent years like this growing up, my mother hovering over my every move, me responding mono-syllabically, face blank, voice blank, heart blank. It is an easy coping mechanism if you are able to block out false promises of love with the understanding of what love has become.

You followed me into the room and grabbed me by the arm. I yanked it away.

"*No*."

That basement was so badly lit, I could not even see the look on your face properly as you grabbed me and pushed me into a sitting position on the ground.

I am a wall. I am a wall. I am a wall.

We wrestled, collapsing with our legs intertwined. Limbs fumbled as you tried to touch my face and I tried to slap you off. I could not look at you. Could not speak. And then, your hand, gentle on my cheek. That feeling of caving I know all too well.

It is my lover who is a wall. A wall with no windows. This morning when she kissed me, she presented me with her brick mouth, tongue of mortar congealing, as if preparing to seal shut the last secret pathway to her heart. She is the wide expanse of the earth placed into moulds, excess scraped off the edges, built box upon box.

I want to open her up, hammer and nail. I want to expose the trap of her mouth filled with lies. I want to scrape out all these omissions from the insides of her cheeks. I want to see what half-eaten alphabets I can find in her throat.

What is her name, this other woman? I want to know. I want to roll it beneath my tongue till I have ground it to pieces

I can sprinkle over you like so much confetti regret. Tell it to me so I can master a new curse word. I want to hear the way her name sounds coming from your mouth. Tell me her name so that if I ever meet her, I can pretend that I have forgotten it.

Unfair, really, how your tears induce mine. You kept asking me the same question over and over. Was there something I needed to say to you? I could not bear to watch you suffer the humiliation I'd suffered the day before at your hands: Me asking if you had betrayed my trust, me watching you deny it.

Betrayal is a tricky thing. Does it exist in the act of treachery, or in the lie that dismisses it? Do we lie because we are careful or because we are cruel? When we are left standing naked, do we regret what we've done, or the fact that we've been found out?

You told me you'd been afraid to hurt me. I told you that you were a coward.

A lie is a lie is a lie is a lie.

STAIRS

THE TWO WEEKS we slept in that basement, I felt as though I had weights tied to my feet. Each time you left for work, I remained downstairs, emerging from darkness only to shower. Occasionally, I ate. Every now and then, I tried to read. But for the most part, I lay in bed, staring at the ceiling or clicking aimlessly through cyberspace.

I found myself watching a lot of movies on YouTube; specifically, films and cartoons that I had watched so many times as a kid, I knew most of the dialogue by heart. There was something easy and sure about this; something familiar about not having to anticipate plot points. I found myself thinking a lot about childhood.

MaaaahhMMEEEEEEEEEE!

This was the daily ritual that befell my household during the holidays, once my mother began her new job at the papers. It was 1990, I was in the afternoon session for school and each day she left for work, I would run to the verandah, hang my legs through the grills and swing them in the air. And then, from 25 storeys in the air:

MaaaahhMMEEEEEEEEEE!

Living on the top floor of a point block was the rage in those days; these new marvels that surpassed their 12-storey sisters in height and eclipsed them in terms of privacy. We towered over the neighbourhood, watched over everything that fell between the basketball courts and the bank. Ang Mo Kio had been built up the year before I was born and prefab flats were valued for their novelty. It was clearly going to be a decade of prosperity. Almost 240,000 flats had been built the decade before, and soon, the entire nation would be living in the sky.

We each had a role to play in our little tower. My grandfather, a retired motorcycle racer who had charmed Malayan hearts back in the 50s, was now a caretaker at a church. His trophies lined our display cabinets and his victories at the Johore Grand Prix remain archived in the national papers. He now took care of a place of worship dedicated to a god he did not believe in, and when no one was looking, stole the umbrellas that people left behind. If it was a particularly quiet day, he would use them to poke at the mangoes that looked just right, attempting to put as many of them into his bag as possible before coming home. Evenings consisted of playing the lottery via teletext and spying on passers-by with his binoculars. He read the news diligently, particularly the obituary section, checking to see if anyone we knew had died. He spoke regularly of the occupation, during which he had been interned. Half-English, half-Japanese, he never spoke of his parents, of the circumstances into which he was born, of how he ended up a composite of two geographies thrust into battle over who owned whom.

My grandmother, too, spoke of the war. Of mass murders at a hospital that took place on the feast of St. Valentine. Of how the Japanese soldiers stormed into the houses of anyone who opposed their dominance, with an aim to correct any non-Japanese women who they might have taken a fancy to. Green-eyed and mahogany-haired, she hid under the bed with her sisters. They covered their faces with charcoal and smeared their bodies with dirt. They wanted to repulse those men the way the men repulsed them. She would not let anyone touch her.

My grandmother lived in the kitchen and, as many women of her time did, waited on my grandfather. She cooked, cleaned, and left her job as a supervisor at the telephone board to raise my uncle, who eventually fled for New Zealand the minute the prospect of conscripted military service arose, and my mother, who, in turn, had me. When my grandfather hollered "Coffee!" from the bedroom, she went to the kitchen to make it. When he yelled "Tea!" from the couch, the pot would be heard boiling in 10 minutes.

By the time I was born, my father was gone. My mother, newly single and born again, loved her five-room flat. She furnished it with kitsch that ranged from trendy, dark wood furniture to miniature clogs she'd bought in Holland. She travelled widely and for free by virtue of being a travel writer, and ate well by virtue of being a food writer. She had decided that she would live a life of the bourgeois that being a disc jockey had not previously afforded her. She aspired to eat at restaurants that offered breadsticks before meals. She wanted to travel to far-flung places, specifically to visit the tourist traps.

She was going to be a god-fearing woman and entrepreneur who believed in both capitalism and Christ.

And then there was me. This racially ambiguous, single-parented, girl-child screaming the height of 25 storeys to meet my mother's ears. My household was generally accommodating, because that was the only noise I made for the day. And once Mother had walked out of eyeline, and I was convinced that my voice could carry through 25 storeys of air, I kept mostly to myself.

Actually, I kept a lot to myself. I did not like other children, hated it when relatives came over, and I often had to be bribed into taking photos. When I was eight years old, one of my teachers asked us about the things we were able to put into sandwiches. *Cheese! Ham! Tuna fish! Peanut butter!* I remember putting up my hand.

Worms, I said.

My teacher raised her eyebrow at me, not convinced. She asked me what sort of worms I thought I was able to eat. She did not know that I spent a lot of time at the shops that sold goldfish in Ang Mo Kio Central, watching owners feed clumps of blood worms to their captives. Pinch-sized tangles of deep red, dumped into the water, separating themselves into thin, wriggling strands. The shops kept their fish in separate plastic bags blown up with oxygen and filled with water. You could watch the goldfish, mouths gaping and eyes wide open, wiggling their ways to the surface of the water to gobble up as much as they could.

When I answered, I left out everything about the fish but described the worms in great detail, telling her that I found them in the drains. I watched as her face transformed from disbelief to disgust. Noises of *eeeeeeeeeee* filled the room. Recess for the next three months comprised eating 40-cent plates of wantan noodles in solitude because none of the other girls would sit with me. Till today, I still enjoy eating out alone.

I never quite fit into the mold of what every Singaporean girl was supposed to be. In church and at piano lessons, I often got into trouble for beating up the boys, and when coming home from playing soccer downstairs, I would get despairing looks from my grandma who would feel compelled to clean my shoes.

On the other hand, I also loved wearing dresses and hairbands, and like many girls, often liked to think myself a princess; not because I wanted to be pretty or have a prince sweep me off my feet, but because I thought that wearing a crown would put me in charge. Kings were boys. And queens were wives of kings. I did not want to get married so being a princess seemed like the only option.

I also enjoyed the opportunities for decoration that princess-dom provided. I enjoyed the fluffy taffeta dresses in all their impracticality, the patent pink shoes and the frilly socks. They would be among the first things to go when I hit 18. Tired of all my classmates telling me to let my hair down, I would take a plastic pink razor to my head and shave it all off. It had not been a neat, clean shave, but one that left tufts of hair on the surface of my head. I remember looking in the mirror and feeling the surface of my scalp under the palms of my hands, feeling with my thumb the dent just above the base of my scalp and gazing upon my face as though seeing myself for the first time. By that time, I'd dropped out of junior college to go to art school and fit the glorious stereotype of the teen no Singaporean parent wants: tattered shirts, paint-stained jeans, no hair, and the first signs of ink.

Femininity was an hour-long ritual that my mother took seriously each day, and she spent much of her time in front of the mirror. She had been a minor celebrity in her time before she had me, hosting game shows on television and disc jockeying on the radio. It was the 80s and that meant beehive hair, shoulder pads, and the one hundred bottles of magic she lined her dresser with. It was an era of ornamentation and my mother longed to be ornamentalised. She left the house, glitter in her hair and on the lids of her eyes, rouge highlighting cheekbones that had once been prominent, perfume that would find your nostrils a mile away.

The need to transform herself escalated into a sort of a body image obsession. And once she realised that time would eventually take her looks from her, she started to panic. Her skin was losing its signature tautness. She was finding it hard controlling her weight. It dawned on her that she was getting on in years and that her marriage had ended. Her life started taking on strange and skewed perspectives marked by beauty products, sell-a-vision, and God.

First, there was the Abdominizer, which helped her *rock, rock, rock her way to a firmer, flatter stomach* a grand total of twice before it was relegated to the storeroom. Then it was the purchasing of beauty products from duty-free, each piled on with such urgency it seemed as though the goal was to erase her face altogether. And then, the slimming treatments, which she took a liking to long before photoshopped models and before-and-after photos became a staple in our newspapers. She had become a body she did not own; a project that needed to be worked on, for which exercise and prayer went hand in hand. She was going to cleanse herself of all things ugly, whether they be love handles or demons. She dieted the way brides-to-be do before weddings. Except that she was going to be a bride of Christ; a woman of her own making, made in the image of God.

I, too, became an ornament. My mother's tangential project. Something that needed to be worthy of being shown off. My weight became a problem. Not for health reasons, but for reasons of appearance. Instead of regulating our excessively Eurasian diet of meat and potatoes, she added another course to the daily meals: slimming pills. Large ovals of dark brown that tasted of hard plastic. They were what she called fat burners. We would eat them together before meals and she was convinced that I would lose weight. I never did.

My mother's primary audience were the friends she met at church and her primary accessory was me. I was spoken about in elevated tones, especially when I got good grades or could play particularly complicated hymns on the piano or violin. Our ability to speak English "as though we were Caucasians" and our obvious interracial heritage turned us into the spectacle my mother so enjoyed being in our predominantly Chinese congregation.

But then again, we fit right in because the church was a spectacle in and of itself. When you walked into the car park, the first thing you saw were rows of expensive-looking cars. One of them belonged, along with the station wagon, to one of our pastors. The last time someone had asked why he needed two vehicles, he said that the station wagon helped to ferry people caught at the bus stop when it rained during Sunday afternoon service. He made a bad joke about being fishers of men and referenced the monsoon season. When you asked why he still needed the other, he just turned red and said that he had much work to do and *God bless you*.

Ours was the first Pentecostal church to arrive on Singaporean shores in the early 30s. Our American pastors did their jobs with much zeal, learning both Tamil and Mandarin in order to reach out to as many "ethnic" sheep as they could. They believed that whatever wealth the church had been blessed with was a reward for the good that was achieved. On the notice board that footed the stairs up to the worship area, a list of the top 20 tithers was pinned up next to notices regarding church camps, in order of the ascending amounts of money donated.

Next to the notice board was the children's area, where kids were taught the finer points of the straight-and-narrow. Activities such as song-and-dance (who can forget the riveting actions to *I Love You Jesus?*) and paper cut-outs were just a few of the days' activities. Memorising the chronology of the books in the New Testament was another. And always, the consequences of sin and the guilt of not loving Jesus enough to do the right thing.

Sunday school was very similar to regular school, meaning I could not really connect with anyone my own age. I was once called into the office for beating up a boy who was 10. He had called me a "fatty-bom-bom" and I had kicked him in the area that no boy should ever be kicked in. I had learned this maneuver from movies I was not supposed to be watching when my mother was at her church meetings. It was used by bad guys on cops, angry girlfriends on boyfriends, and wrestlers who liked to play dirty. To add to the misdemeanour, I had not stopped there. Upon seeing him hunched over, I took the opportunity to pummel him with my fists.

"Aren't *you* skeptical," sniffed a Sunday School teacher, when I asked how she knew God wanted us to follow the Bible. After all, it was written thousands of years ago—maybe God had changed his mind about some things? When I remembered the comment as an adult, I laughed, and imagined myself popping out of my mother's womb with furrowed eyebrows, looking doubtful.

What a stupid thing to say to a child.

I was never quite convinced that if I walked through fire, I would not get burned. Nor that if I got bitten by poisonous snakes, I would not die. People died from fires every day and I was pretty sure that at least a few of them were Christians.

These opinions did not leave me well liked by the Sunday School teachers.

"We are not supposed to do these things on purpose. There is a difference between faith and stupidity. We trust God. We do not test Him."

"My grandmother told me that Mother Teresa touched the wound of a leper and put her fingers on her tongue to show her faith. Isn't *that* testing?"

"I hear that your grandmother is not saved. She is Catholic, right? They are different from us. Thy pray to Mary and bow before statues. We worship the one true God."

"But my grandmother prays to Jesus."

"But that won't save her from hell. Why don't you try bringing her to church instead of asking so many questions. I am sure she is old, and does not have much time left."

I went home and sat in my grandmother's lap. I said nothing about the exchange. I buried my face in her neck. She smelled of lavender.

My grandmother was really the person who held our family together. My best memories of home centre around her. It was with her I learned how to join the dots, play Snakes and Ladders, Solitaire. Always from her came stories about my grandfather's brother who had climbed up a cherry tree to pee on his ex-girlfriend and her new boyfriend when they paused under it to kiss. Being with her always calmed me, and her running her fingers through my hair always induced sleep. She remained Catholic till the year I turned twelve . . . but that is for later, when things start to come apart.

I have fewer positive memories of my mother, all of them relegated to early childhood: cotton candy at Parco Funworld where you could sit in Viking rides that hurled your stomach into your throat, Sunday excursions to the second-hand bookstore at Serangoon Gardens, ice-jelly at the wet market nearest to our flat. And most of the time, even these remain eclipsed by force-fed sessions of the Bible, a daily ritual behind closed doors that took on a dark and heavy quality as the years passed; multiple music lessons every week with unhappiness for anything less than Distinctions. Being left on the tour bus in Thailand while she filled bags full of souvenirs; the tour guide closing the doors of the bus, and sitting me on his knees. The hardness that sprang from between his legs as he rocked me back and forth across his lap. His laughter and his yellow teeth.

One particular memory remains clear: 11 years old. I was in the back seat of a car belonging to my mother's friend. All four of us had just descended what seemed like a long flight of staircases—eight storeys? Nine?—I can't remember. I just recall thinking that the journey down had seemed far easier than the journey up. And that my mother was voicing her regret at having worn such high heels on a day the elevator had decided to break down.

We had just come back from sitting in a flat with two men, who had probably been in their early 30s. Handsome, well-spoken, and smiling. I was fawned over and patronised by one, while the other brought my mother and her friend, a real-estate agent, tea.

So, should I help them sell?
I don't know. How do you feel?
They are living in sin. But they have been good clients.
Maybe you have been sent here to turn them.
I am so confused.
Maybe we should pray about it.

And they did.

Hearing that exchange as a child felt a lot like listening to two people reference you in a conversation that you were not a part of, in a language that you did not understand—there was a barrier between what I felt and my ability to understand why I felt it. The feeling of that memory never left me, disconcerting me at every turn for reasons I was yet unable to name. It unfolded itself gradually, until from within it, a sense of rejection, unmistakable, revealed itself like a rotting core. Until today, when that memory revisits, I often change the ending, imagining my child-self opening the door of that car and walking out. The same way I've done decisively so many times since then with jobs, conversations, people. Once they start getting unpleasant, they become situations that must be abandoned. Habits like this die hard.

But our parents never leave. The ones who gave us names, fed us, clothed us, put language in our mouths and limits around our hearts. We are able to separate ourselves from them as much as we are able to disentangle ourselves from the genes that dictated the colour of our eyes and the texture of our hair.

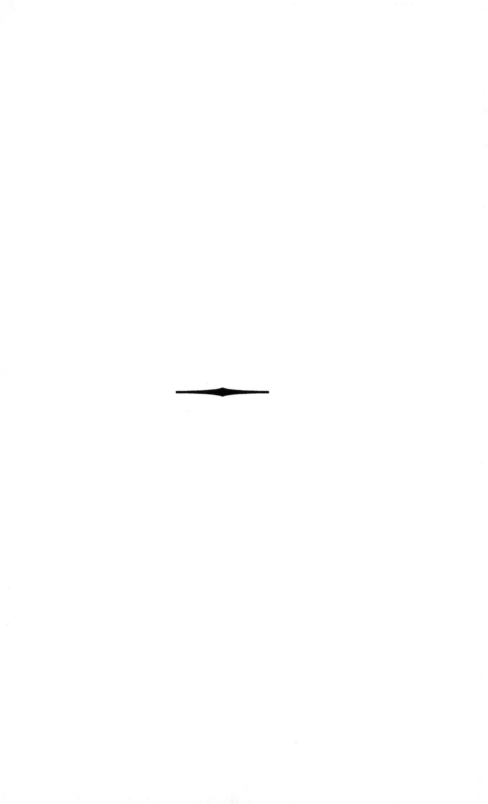

DRAWERS

THERE IS AN article in this week's *New Paper* about convent schools, proposing that all-girl secondary schools turn teenage girls into lesbians. It is front-page news. It is baiting readers with a large colour photo of two girls in blue pinafores, faces pixellated, sitting at a bus stop and cuddling. The word *Lesbian* is in large, 3-centimetre, Arial font, sharp and straight, the way all teenage girls apparently should be.

I am 13. It is the first time I have seen the word *lesbian* in print. I keep the article underneath the photo albums in the bottom drawer of my desk. I will see the word again three months later in a novel called *Ruby* that I borrow from the school library. It is from that book that I also learn the word *dyke*. Either the selection that came into the library had not been properly vetted, or the librarian knew that a girl like me would read a book like that and slipped it, compassionately, through the cracks.

The tabloid, of course, had its own ludicrous repercussions within school walls. Girls who sported undercuts were threatened with wigs. Girls caught holding hands or acting intimately would get sent straight to counselling. The resident counselor, in fact, took the liberty of making an announcement in front of the whole school during Monday assembly about how we were not going to turn into an institution that "produced lesbians".

Of course, not all the girls in school bothered with the new rules.

The day after the counselor recited her ode to homophobia at assembly, which included the perils of girls with hair cut like boys, Alex, two years my senior (and perhaps what some might have called "the school stud") returned to class with her initials shaved into the side of her head. We gushed and gawked and giggled. She wore her disdain for the status quo in the belt that fell upon her hips instead of her waist; in the silver that ran down one ear; and I, too, in my adolescent imitation of what has been, till today, an unapologetic contempt for dress codes.

She was beautiful, and she walked with a swagger that all of us, at one point or another, either out of jest or admiration, tried to imitate. She taught us that it was ok to have an opinion and to wear it like a medal. She scored three-pointers on the court the same way she scored straight A's in class, and she looked as good in her debate uniform, starched and skirty, as she did in the hard denims she wore to town.

I used to think I was in love with her, even though I barely knew her. I now know that what I loved was what she represented. She taught me, simply by being herself, that I should be unapologetic about who I was.

Love would come three years later. I was chairperson of the drama society, which meant that everything was cause for drama. She was captain of the badminton team, which meant that she ran circles around me with perfect poise. This would set the pattern of our relationship over the next four years: high emotion, high drama, two lives once separate, now revolving around each other at breakneck speed.

I had wanted to become an activist because at the time, I thought this was an actual profession. She wanted to join the U.N. and work towards ending world hunger. Neither of us would end up doing either of these things, but at sixteen, they were as real as undone homework and canteen lunch. I brought her home to meet my mother. Mother called her my "good friend".

For months, every day, my house or hers. Bags. Files. Books. Paper. Four pairs of limbs and chalk-white shoes. Uniform cotton. Mid-afternoon heat. Pinafore pleats conspiring and crumpled, collar unbuttoned, convent blue from shoulders to knees, caught halfway between ocean and sky, wallet dragging material pocket-down, the entire uniform perpetually lopsided.

And that was me, summed up. Sixteen and lopsided. Lopsided hair, lopsided anger, the lopsided smile friends now note to be specifically reserved for women I'm attracted to. Lopsided in love, as I have been ever since. Diving headfirst with no second thoughts.

And it was the way they always say it is. Every cliché in the book. If she was the sun, I was Icarus in love. If she was the stars, I was a story mapped out. If she was a tornado, I was Dorothy, lifted, house and all, and dumped promptly into a saturated reality not my own. I was outside myself, beside myself, all feeling and no words with which to explain what had just happened. She was an alternate universe and the beginning of language.

In the beginning was the word and the word was *God* and she was the word. She bade light and the night lifted from my eyes. She bade life and my heart teemed with all manner of things that galloped, crawled, swam, ran, howled at the moon. She said *up* and tongued skies in the roof of my mouth; she said *down*, and without blinking, drew oceans from my body with the tip of a finger.

She was the word. And then *we* were the words. Hello. Goodbye. Now. Wait. Please. No. Yes. Don't. Hear. Sshhh. Come. Go. You. Me. Us. Love. Every word was new. Every word had weight. Everything that came from her mouth was something holy I could live on and feast on and pray to until I was whole.

We wrote each other letters. Spoke late into the night. Passed each other notes in class. There was never nothing to say to each other. Even in silence, text reshaping itself onto our faces and under our skin.

The first time we kissed, words spilled out of mouths and into each other's throats.

I choked on them and cried for an hour.

Lesbian.

I thought of the article at the bottom of my drawer.

Who knew the act of speaking could hurt so much? Could hold in its mouth that one concrete thing which gives weight to questions you never thought to ask, and shape to answers you never thought you'd find? Leaving the womb a second time, crying, because that's what we all do the day we're born.

And then, words of comfort. Whispered words. Words on palms in the flick of her wrist, behind the lids of her eyes.

On stage, we played various characters, ran amok and annoyed directors. At school debates, we argued on the same team, wore power jackets and black heels. In class, we slept on our tables and on the bus, we held hands at the back seat. Head on shoulder, sleep-talk, nicknames, code words. She was oblivious to the stares and for that, I was glad.

Uniform cotton mid-afternoon heat. Ridding ourselves of bags and shoes. Two of us in my room beneath the planks of my double-decker bed, blue shedding like skin, white undershirts flimsy and translucent. Undoing her belt. Pushing pleats above bent knees.

The first time I entered her, I found a place inside myself in which I no longer needed to speak. She kissed me, exhaled, breathed in so hard I thought she might inhale me whole: lips, teeth, tongue, tonsils, lining of throat. She gave language to a silence I'd not known was even there. She gave language to my body, undeveloped. She gave language to me, still teething on amorphous ideas about love, desire, longing, and sex.

When she got married years later, her sister gave the speech, and gesturing to the bride and groom, announced that each had been the other's first love. My best friend and I sat hand in hand in silence, watching words wipe away in three seconds what we'd taken years to master.

You never realise how personal notions of history are until yours has been erased.

The day she left, I lay on my bed and looked up at the planks that supported the upper deck. Every time she'd stayed over, she'd left me a note written on the wood. Words in coloured markers I could stare at like stars. Text-coded, over-lapping, hugging edges, incomplete. I wrote my own in a locked diary stashed up in a cupboard beneath the plastic holder of my Monopoly set. Words sitting uncomfortably between miniature houses, paper money, and a sign that told me not to pass *GO*.

I still keep her letters in a box, in the bottom drawer, much like the way I kept that tabloid article about convent school lesbians. I keep them to remind myself of how important it is that I write my own history. And because I like remembering a time when words meant something. When words were promises and not excuses, truth and not fact, bridges that link one human being to another instead of the walls that keep them apart.

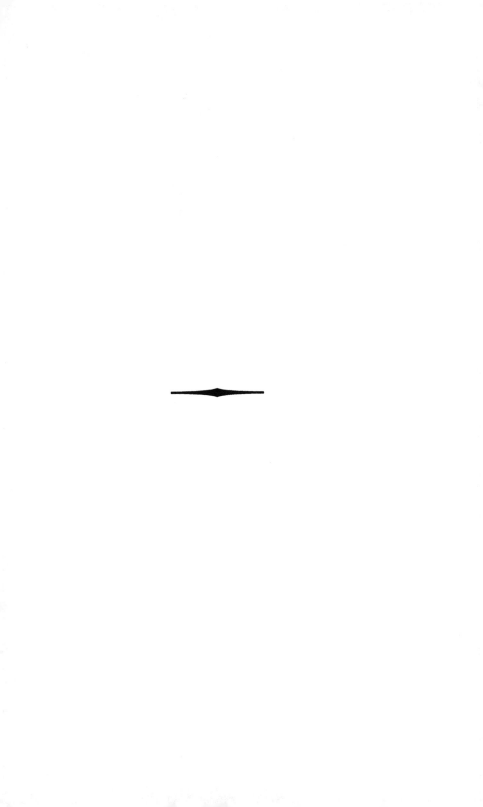

BED

IT'S ALMOST MIDNIGHT and I've just responded to a booty call. One of those you *know* you should not respond to. A rebound relationship that went up in flames. Three months of not seeing each other had been successfully enforced. Till we met again at a civil society event and I somehow ended up in her bed.

Fine. I did not "somehow end up in her bed". She asked me back to her place, and I went. But only after a two-hour conversation about how that would be a bad idea, us initially taking separate cabs and me eventually redirecting mine.

So here I am again, in yet another taxi, high-heeled, lip-glossed, hair-primped. Emotionally, I feel as though I've been hollowed out, so I am happy to coast through the next few months at the mercy of my hormones and her whims. You suggested I go look for someone else. I didn't. But found someone anyway.

The attraction is rather befuddling. I don't know whether it is the depth of her voice or the length of her legs. Or the fact that she has a small library in her living room and an even larger one in her head. She enjoys bestowing me with fun facts. Like how ethnicity is virtually untraceable when you flay someone completely. Or how dimples are just undeveloped muscle. Or how you cannot really tell what direction sound is coming from if you are lying horizontally. Her ability to cross-reference feminist texts is making it worse. But then again, maybe I am just horny and all I really want is a good grope and a long romp in the sack.

She is quick to identify what makes me tick, and this is part of the draw. Quips fly quickly back and forth. I've never been a fan of smooth-talkers, but today, this is exactly what I need. When they're this swift at seduction, they've done it before:

Things are simple when you know you're not special.

———

What do these people do in bed, the preacher chides, *except make a mockery of the bodies God has given us?*

Not again, I think to myself, sitting in the last pew. Having graduated from Sunday School, I am barely a year into adult services when I decide that I have heard this line of questioning one too many times. I wonder if my scowl is visible from all the way up front. To my left, a preacher's daughter with a penchant for late nights at clubs. To my right, a fourteen-year-old who will get pregnant in another two months and extricate herself from services altogether. Besides clearly not fitting in with the rest of the congregation, we had nothing in common really, beyond that back pew and beyond consistently excusing ourselves halfway through service to go eat *chee chong fan* across the street.

The church today, with its elaborate stained glass and air-conditioned premises, is very different from the church I remember. We were once a series of modest, plain white concrete buildings and containers. That is, till the fire hit. That is when the rebuilding began.

We did not know where to start with the renovation, the pastor proclaimed. *But now, God has given us a sign!*

The ability to be positive in the face of a fire that had consumed half the premises was admirable.

The church's pastors arrived in Singapore in the late 1920s on the heels of an evangelical movement that had emerged in Arkansas; a movement that would soon grow to encompass 60 million people around the world. We were told that we were not so much a denomination as a fellowship. We had been called together to be one with Christ. By the 70s, the missionaries from America had created missionaries from Singapore. The church prospered quietly alongside the nation, and in the 80s, I became part of the congregation.

The rhetorical questions of "what these people do in bed" were often succeeded by "God made Adam and Eve, not Adam and Steve". These were the token adages thrown out at every sermon that involved describing the sins of our times. Creating sinners is much like creating terrorists: Pick an invisible enemy and fan the flames of fear. Our head pastors were still making those jokes the day I attended church for the last time.

Ironically, it was their words, combined with enrolling at a convent school in which many girls paired off, that made me ask the same question: What *do* they do in bed?

My mother had saved herself the sex talk by giving me Peter Mayles's *Where Did I Come From?* in kindergarten. All the things that book left out, she did not supplement. So when the preacher started asking those questions, so did I.

Believe me, my mother said. *They are wicked, they find ways.*

What do I do in bed? How is that anyone's business but mine?

"You make very good pasta," he said to my breasts. I cringed, but managed to avoid rolling my eyes.

"Thank you," I said, reminding myself that living with a housemate meant accommodating her friends when they came over. I am not a people person and I am not a politician and I hated myself for being polite. I continued moving the devilled eggs from the Tupperware to the serving tray. The sounds of a long night partying ahead filled the kitchen, even though we were the only two people there. I could not wait to get back outside. I doubled my preparation speed. I cursed at the yolk that was dribbling down the side of my forearm.

"Your future husband will be a very lucky man," he said, slurring his words from one too many whiskies and way too many assumptions. By now, I was biting my tongue so hard I was surprised that I had not drawn blood. Hadn't this joker come with his wife?

Where the fuck was she? I put down the eggs for a second so that I could finish my beer. Perhaps time would go faster if I was as drunk as him. My friend, Chris, came into the kitchen, looking for another Pilsner, and saw me glugging.

"You mean my *wife*, don't you? You met my *girl*friend in the living room just now, right?" He furrowed his eyebrows quizzically, like a small boy who had just realised that he was not the centre of the universe. Except that this forty-year-old child was making me lose my patience quickly. One more tray of eggs and I would be out of there.

"But how do you decide on who is the husband and who is the wife?"

Chris slammed the refrigerator door and stood behind him, opening her mouth to say something. I grabbed her wrist and asked whether she could help me take the first tray of eggs out to the guests. She yanked it out of my hands, asking me whether I was ok. I nodded, turning back to the man who clearly still thought that my face was on my chest.

"There is no husband. We are both women and that is it." I picked up the tray. Everything was done. His *"But if..."* trailed off into the distance as I re-emerged in the living room, bearing eggs.

For the next two hours, the night moved on as planned. Alcohol was consumed, cigarettes smoked. Our housemate's friends staked territory in the living room while ours occupied the dining area. It was my fifth apartment and it was cause for celebration. All three of us loved the apartment and so did the cats who spent their afternoons stretching out across windowsills and lounging on the sofa. Any apartment I occupied for more than three months was a celebration. I had, over the past few years, garnered a reputation for my constant moving, so we toasted to a long stay.

We were on the second storey of a walk-up in Hougang and it was beautiful. It did not matter that nothing matched. That three glossy fortune gods looked upon Formica working spaces. That dirty wooden easels stood upon polished marble floors. That the retro furniture we had picked up from a void deck in Bedok clashed terribly with the modern monstrosities that matched only each other. That the toilet constantly clogged. That the whole area lived with an underground roach problem so severe that I once heard my housemate screaming from two blocks away, slamming the windows shut as hundreds of them climbed the exterior walls of the apartment, trying to get away from the fumigation downstairs.

For a while, it would be home. And this was a housewarming. There was pasta and cheesecake and fruit salad and potatoes. And there were, of course, devilled eggs. Besides that short encounter in the kitchen, nothing had gone wrong. By 1:00 a.m., I was as high as a kite, washing my hands in the bathroom, steadying myself over the sink, when I heard his voice again, coming from outside the door. He was talking to my housemate.

Her friends are all so hot. Pity they're not really women.

I stopped. Looked in the mirror at my own face. My eyes were bloodshot. I was drunk. There was no way I'd actually heard that. I shook off the shock and turned off the tap.

What the fuck do you mean by that?

It was you. I could hear from your voice that you'd had a lot to drink. I barged out of the toilet.

Get out of my house.

The entire apartment went silent. My housemate stood wide-eyed and motionless. Those who had heard what he said, whispered it to the person sitting next to them. His words had lacked nuance, but we knew exactly what they meant. So many of us had heard these sorts of refrains so many times, and when he attempted to backtrack, chaos ensued.

Everyone got in on it—it was as though there stood an invisible camel in the room whose back had been broken by that man's words. When everyone eventually ran out of things to say and silence found us waiting for a response, he tried to reconcile matters by telling me (again) that he liked my pasta and that he hoped I would make it again for him someday.

More chaos.

The night ended.

In tears.

His.

Trying to explain himself to my housemate the next day, he said that he had just been curious about what lesbians do in bed. Who was the guy? Who was the girl? Who does what? She defended him.

Funny. When he had walked into the house with his wife, I felt no desire to find out who got on top.

I considered my housemate for a second, overwhelmed by a sudden conclusion:

The next time I move, I do it alone.

———

I look at my phone. There's still time to go back. The price of a reroute would simply be a naggy complaint from a driver who finds out he might not be able to cruise into midnight fare after all.

But at the apartment, she is wearing a white shirt with blue stripes. She runs one hand up my thigh before I have time to shut the door. We wrestle over who is in charge, and just when I think I have her, she has me pinned to the wall by my wrists.

She is a tall tale of pleasure I would like to tell, spinning out from between my legs. She carves out moans from the deep of my bones. She loads me like a gun, wanting to fire me into the sky. And when she is rough, I feel centuries leak from the corners of my eyes. I want her to want me enough to take me hard. We might not see each other again once this is done but that's a long way away and all I know is now.

———————

Make no mistake about what we do in bed. We aren't big-haired actors, hands all over each other, casting you side glances from between the sheets. We aren't the pig-tailed schoolgirls in thigh-high socks you think about while your wife gives you your monthly blowjob. And forget, most of all, the picket-fenced women of the L-word who make out in filtered light to commissioned music. All you have to know is that my lover never goes limp and that I never leave unsatisfied. That neither of us is thinking about men. That neither of us is thinking about you.

Sometimes, she straddles my waist, wearing only her jeans, my wrists and ankles restrained to the bed. Tied up, I feel an immense relinquishing of power so liberating and filled with so much trust, I want to melt myself into some sort of liquid and drown both of us in this creature we create. Together, we are a fire and she is a phoenix rising from the ashes of my body. We consume each other and each is killed, reborn, intertwined forever with the coming and going of desire.

I like it when she pulls my hair, when she digs her teeth deep into my skin, when she rubs the wet of her wanting up against my thigh. I like it when she zips her pants down, touches herself and pushes her fingers into my mouth. I like it when she lets me push my tongue deep into her, lets me taste that sweet salty sap; when the whole world shrinks down to the space between my mouth and her clit; when she is about to come, body beautiful and hard like some sort of mathematical puzzle waiting to be solved.

When I arrive at her door, she whispers in my ear. Says that by the time she is done with me, I am not going to remember my own name.

She asks if I want it, and I say yes.
And it is true. This is all I want.

––––––

Beds were originally shallow holes dug into the ground and covered with grass. From their dimensions, archaeologists have concluded that our ancestors slept in fetal positions. I still do that when I am trying to get back in touch with myself. I guess all of us, at some point want to return to our first homes.

After a decade at sea, lost, in battle with gods and having to deal with incompetent men who forgot their own homecoming, it was finally their marriage bed that brought Odysseus and Penelope back together. With skin weathered like paper and eyes weary from years of both earthly and transcendental wars, Penelope did not recognise him. It was only when he told her that their bed was made from an olive tree still rooted to the ground, that she truly understood that her lover had returned.

When you and I lay in our first bed, sex was never a problem. Sleeping, on the other hand, was an issue. We had not had the money to afford more than a single bed and the only thing worse than tossing and turning is tossing and turning in a space with no space.

We would sleep in many beds afterwards. Paper-thin *tilams* you would find on the streets of Amsterdam made for half a person, but which would fit both of us and an insistent cat. The double we would eventually get, paintings stored beneath its wooden planks. Or the bed we first slept in, in the studio I shared with another painter; an Ikea fold-out topped with a mattress so worn we could feel the planks of wood complaining against the muscles in our backs. The single bed in your childhood room the night your family went on vacation in Malaysia — sound of the newspaper man making his rounds in the heartlands, the cupboards lined with basketball comics and Xiao Ding Dang figurines.

Bedsheets were the first domestic item we bought together. Black with maroon prints. Half-price at Junction 8. They were queen-sized even though our bed was a single. The logic was that once we were able to afford a larger bed, these sheets would still fit. The sort of logic passed down from grandmothers who insisted on school uniforms being three sizes too large; on hems that they could take in, undoing them as we grew taller.

We knotted the corners of the sheets, and tightened them around the bed. It was the start of a life in which nothing would ever match. We clipped scraps of cloth to rods and made curtains. We covered boxes in old clothes and used them as tables. We ignored the smell of the new paint on the walls and put the first poster up in the living room.

———

I have cried enough for now.

That is my first thought as I wake up. I must have been dreaming of something harsh. What sort of thought is that to have, first thing in the morning?

Her fingers are in my hair. It's a toss between getting to the library early, as I'd planned, and letting the motions of her hand against my head lull me back to sleep the same way they woke me up. It is clear that 7:00 a.m. is not my time of day. I turn around to find her smiling at me. Her body is dappled with morning light. She finds my morning squint amusing. And I can tell by her expression that I've got muppet hair. I bury my head into her neck, letting out a little whine.

"It's so bright," I complained.

"It's called sunlight," she laughed. "How late were you up last night?"

"4:30 a.m." I like to catch up on work after midnight.

"You should get more sleep," she says, hand moving from the back of my head to my face.

71

Staying awake is a losing battle. Staying out of trouble is an even harder one. That one-night stand carried on for a year, though we never cared for each other the way real couples do. It was hard explaining the temporality to friends; the willingness to be part of something we both acknowledged was a passing phase. Sometimes when I woke in the middle of the night and looked at her face, I wanted to tell her that when I think about our relationship, I imagine the sound of a pebble falling into a well so deep that you never get to hear the splash. That on occasion, when she takes my hand, I feel as if I am holding a foreign object.

She kissed me on the forehead. Had you seen us at that very moment, I would not have been able to convince you of the fact that we weren't actually in love. I would not have been able to convince you of the fact that, yes, we sometimes find great tenderness with strangers.

"Sorry," I say, eyes closing.

"What are you sorry for . . ."

DOORS

"SOMEONE'S IN THE house."

I know the sound is not my imagination because you're sitting up straight just like me, body tense. It takes me awhile to decipher your expression. We have no windows in this room and my eyes are having trouble adjusting. I want to flip a switch so that the lights go on, but there aren't any switches by our bed.

It was a loud sound. Short and sharp. Like a big something hitting the ground quickly. Or snapping into two very large pieces. Like a gunshot. Except we don't have guns here. If you're murdered in Singapore, it's usually stab wounds; an intimate violence.

"Someone's in the house," I say again, as if we didn't hear me the first time.

When I am going through a bad period in my life, no matter what it may concern, I have a recurring nightmare that revolves around this. Someone is coming into a space that is supposed to be safe. The idea fills me with unbearable fear: Come rob me of a lifetime of worldly possessions while I am out. Come plunder the last of my paintings and set them afire. Rewire my computer, change the locks on my bedroom door, steal my change, my ID, my electronics . . . just be gone by the time I get back.

"Are you sure?" You're getting out of bed. I pull you back down.

"Are you crazy? You're not going out there!"

Suddenly, the rest of our home that was not our bedroom had become *out there*. Unknown. Outside. Wilderness.

I make a move to get up.

Is the bedroom door locked?

Yes. Her turn to pull me down. *You're not going out there.*

If you go, I go. You want?

No.

So?

No one taught us that this would always be the hardest role to negotiate. We took turns cooking. We took turns cleaning. We both did the heavy lifting and painted the walls. You unclogged the toilet. I washed up after parties. You dealt with the roaches. I camouflaged messes when people came over. We both bought clothes that did not require ironing and neither of us put enough stock in what was on the television to get ours fixed.

But who was going to be the one who allowed the other to walk out first? These were pants neither would let the other wear. Who in their right mind would let their lover meet danger head-on while lingering in the back? In the movies, it is assumed that the men leave the bedroom with a golf club or a baseball bat. How do women cope with that?

In those dreams, I am usually in some sort of interior space. With only one entrance, and someone trying to get through that entrance. The dream has taken place in elevators, in homes, in classrooms. Always, I am trying to bolt a latch or press the elevator door shut or climb out the window of a high-rise to hide. But the person always gets through. And I know that I am finished. And that is when the dreams ends. I never actually get to see what I am sure is my own death.

"I think it's your mother," you say, as we walk through the supermarket. You pop a carton of yoghurt into the cart. "The fact that she was always going through your things."

"What do you mean?"

"The fact that you liked to keep your bedroom door shut."

"Doesn't everyone?"

"Has any friend you've ever lived with kept their room door shut *all* the time?"

"I like my privacy."

"At the expense of ventilation."

"There are windows."

"You leave them closed."

"I don't want roaches."

"What's the point of doors if you don't leave them open?"

"What's the point of doors if they can't be closed?"

When the Swiss were digging up ground for Zurich's opera house, they discovered a door that was five thousand years old and almost perfectly intact. It was said to be part of a community of stilt houses in which you would rarely ever find anything aboveground that was intact. It was created around the same time as Stonehenge, and in many ways, was almost as wondrous.

Climates at the time were harsh. People needed doors that kept the wind out. The area in which the door had been found must have been particularly susceptible, located across from

Lake Zurich, where winds must have raced across the sur-
faces of water, full of invisible teeth in search of warm flesh to
bite into.

When I first left home, I kept the keys to my mother's
house with me all the time. Even when I stopped going back to
steal food mid-afternoons. Even when I stopped going back
to see my grandmother.

I would move house seven times over the next four years.
Doubled rents, evil housemates, cruel landlords, termites. The
reasons would differ but the situation remained the same—
housing on your own terms requires either money or moving.
I had no money, so I moved. And each time I moved, I added
keys to my collection.

Doors, gates, mailboxes, bedrooms, storerooms, drawers.
After I hit about 30 keys, still able to differentiate one from
another, which key went into which drawer on which shelf in
which house before which move, I acknowledged that the
situation was getting out of hand. They were weighing down
my bag, I was running out of connecting key rings and the
jingle-jangle of nomadic history was ringing a little too loud in
my ears. I was too young to be thinking of nicknames like
"Crazy Key Lady".

"Why do you keep them?"

"To remind myself of where I have been."

The minute I discarded them, however, taking the current
keys from the collection and leaving the rest in a drawer, I lost
them as easily as I had collected them. A big clunk of history
stored away in some house I used to live in. For a moment, it

occurred to me that I would never be able to get back into my mother's house again without having to speak to my family, which meant I would probably never see my grandmother again. I felt a tinge of regret, but like my relationship to so many houses, it was short-lived.

I remember, in my second apartment, opening the door to find you carrying a typewriter in your hands. We had spotted it at the Thieves Market on Sungei Road and it had been a beauty. I loved typewriters; the way they looked, the way they sounded when used. The limited pace enforced by the weight of the keys, encouraging the brain to breathe between words.

But 30 dollars back then had been a luxury I could not afford. I did not actually need a typewriter. I already had a second-hand desktop which worked most of the time, and had gotten around a lack of internet connection by traveling to the local library each day. Buying a typewriter would be a little like buying into the same formula used to sell vintage clothes and Polaroid cameras.

I remember opening the door and you standing there, typewriter encased in ochre yellow, hair plastered to your forehead, smile the size of the world. We stood at that doorway for half an hour, because I would not let you in. How could you have undermined my basic philosophy with regard to money? Spend only what is yours, and yours is only what you earn. I hadn't bought that typewriter because I had not been able to afford it. I was so angry at you, even *I* did not know why.

And then, tears growing in the corners of your eyes. Falling onto your T-shirt still drenched from rain. Was I really not going to let you in? Was I really going to leave you standing at the door?

Silence for the next 10 minutes. There was no way someone was moving around a house this old without making a squeak. All I could hear was the sound of us breathing and the thumping of my heart in my throat. If someone was there, how the hell did they make it up the back? Our house was joined to our neighbours'.

"Aiyah," you suddenly exclaimed, voice light. "I think it's the ceiling."

"What?" The sudden change of mood was disorienting me. I saw you getting back into bed.

"The ceiling. That little part warping in the kitchen."

"What, you think it caved in?"

"Yeah, that's probably it."

"Oh you're right. Thank God," I pulled the sheets back around me.

You know you have your shit together when the ceiling of your house is caving in but you really don't mind; when you'd rather wait till morning to deal with whatever might have come down with it. I can't remember any point in my life in which I felt stronger or more capable than I did the next morning, discovering that, no, it had not been the ceiling caving in, but instead, a foosball table that a friend had stored in our kitchen. She had leaned it up against the wall, and for whatever reason, it had fallen down flat onto the ceramic tiles, shattering a few.

The kitchen roof caving in. That I could deal with in the morning. An intruder. That is a whole other story. The front door was intact. The back door was intact. Our bedroom door was intact. Both of us were safe.

ROOF

2006. MY GRANDMOTHER sits in her wheelchair, eyes on the television set. She sees moving images but does not understand them. She rocks back and forth, frail hands clutching armrests. She calls out random words to Warina who comforts her with random words in return. Now and then, when I sneak home to see her, she does not recognise me. She has aged more years than I've been gone.

Three years have passed since I moved out from my mother's flat. But perhaps, "moved" is not an accurate term. It's not like I packed all my belongings into cardboard boxes, sealed them with tape, and stacked them in a van. No. I carried things out bit by bit, a few items each day, in plastic bags. Each day, I placed them into my new house until there was nothing left to carry.

And then, without a word, I just never came back.

Anything that I could not lug myself, I found a way to do without.

Items prioritise themselves quickly when you have limited resources and only one pair of hands.

Six years old. My grandmother would carry my schoolbag while she waited with me for the school bus. Rats inhabited the drain nearby. As a child, I thought it was always the same rat. I used to wait eagerly for it to come out. I called it Rodney.

My grandmother, or *Nana*, as I called her, was disgusted at the idea that I could name a rat.

Nana can't carry anything now, not even what's left of her own weight. She wears diapers, and calls Warina *Mother*. She shouts it loudly so that it can be heard throughout the flat. She shouts it during breakfast, from the dining room that links all our bedroom doors. She shouts it, rocking back and forth, pushing away the food any of us try to feed her.

They say that when a child is born, the parent looks after it and that when the parent grows old, the child returns the favour. "Asian values" positions this as an obligation instead of an act of love. Is it my duty to bear forever the burden of someone else's choice?

I was born an only child. My parents split while my mother was pregnant and my father committed suicide nine years later. I'd never met him and it was an unfelt loss as my mother lay crying in my arms. All I knew of him was what I'd find combing through my mother's drawers years later: divorce papers denoting adultery, photos he'd taken of her on their honeymoon, a scrapbook she had made for him as a teenager.

I am making my parents sound almost human. Perhaps they were, once. My father sailed the seas for work and my mother put pen to paper. My Scorpio parents who made me, the Pisces; twin fishes swimming in circles and never stopping.

When my mother grew tired of dealing with life, she too killed herself, in order to get reborn. This involved joining a Neo-Pentecostal church, much to my grandmother's Roman Catholic despair. There was war every day over whether the statue of the Infant Jesus was a dirty idol or an emblem of faith. My mother always won because we all lived under her roof. That we lived *under her roof* would in fact dictate a number of tyrannies that would eventually define puberty. Even though we lived in a flat, which had only a ceiling and no roof.

So it was decided unilaterally that the Infant Jesus was a dirty idol, and my grandmother would weep as she put the statue back into the cupboard. She did this so that my mother would stop shouting and I would stop crying. And then, each of us to our own retreats: Mother in the room with her Bible; me in my room with my colour pencils; Nana in the kitchen, over the stove.

When I think of Nana, I think of food. Why is it that we so often associate cooking with our grandmothers? I remember with clarity her shepherd's pie, her spaghetti, her devil's curry. I think about the hours I would spend in the kitchen, watching her go about making magic with raw ingredients. All good smells lead back to her.

Thirteen years old. I shunned cooking as a symbol of backwardness. I was going to be a liberated woman who was not tied to her stove. I spent a large portion of my teenhood proud of the fact that I could not boil an egg. I thought this made me a modern woman. I loved it that people were appalled.

An empty bank account, rented house, and stolen pot later, I faced the stove without a choice. How could I have known that cooking would be the final act that liberated me?

Over the course of two decades, meals with my family got worse and worse. When my grandmother lost everything that helped her make sense of the world, my mother felt compelled to compensate for the silences that befell the table. She chattered endlessly of her successes, her clients, and her virtues, and after each proclamation, gave thanks to God. To this day, I find it difficult talking about myself and the life I have made. I would readily choose the sound of cutlery clicking its tongue against plates over having to deal with her voice in my throat.

It was a matter of time before my grandmother grew too deaf to hear her, and I just learned to eat fast and leave. Three generations of women at one table, all held together by blood and excuses and this metaphorical roof above our heads. Dinner after dinner, day after day, year after year. I destroyed that thread. Pulled it so tight, it broke. Or rather, that thread tied itself too tight around me and I, I broke.

I remember the day I knew I wanted to leave.

Seventeen years old. In the hospital. Nana had suffered a stroke and I was by her bed. She was semi-conscious, drugged, unable to speak, half her face unable to emote. Suddenly, phantoms of people I'd known from church, moving in masses, descended upon her bed. She could not have known what was going on. *Thank God*, they repeated, that she was alive. *Praise God*, they said, for sparing her. They began to pray. Their prayers grew with their passions.

I dragged my mother to a corner.

I'm going to leave, I said, if they didn't. They were causing a ruckus, voices inflated with ego, not spirit. People were staring and I was gigantic with rage. The nurse was at a loss and did not know what to do. Nana was distressed.

Or maybe it was I who was distressed. Twelve years old again. Grabbed and pulled into my bedroom. The glazed look in my grandmother's eyes as she sat at the dining table. She'd crushed a framed image of The Last Supper with a hammer they had given her. Mother telling me that Nana had been saved, before they started shouting at me, pulling at my clothes, telling me that demons possessed my body and that they had to be cast out.

Unnatural tendencies, they told my mother. They spoke the word *lesbian* as if it was dirty. And then, my room stripped bare of belongings, and put to flames upon our stove. I snarled and struggled and screamed but they annulled my rage: All resistance was the devil and nothing was mine.

Have these people not known anger? It is not of the devil. I possess it; it does not possess me. If there is only one thing left that I own, it is that. It sits at the core of who I am and you may never cast it out.

In the hospital ward, I felt something in me die. My mother and I, standing at arm's length, glaring at each other. *Last chance*, I thought. I would have forgiven her everything had she picked me.

Would have forgiven her for choosing so many times, book over blood, dogma over daughter.

Choose me. I belong to you. I am more than the myth of some made-up story. I am flesh. I am blood. I am yours. Choose *me*.

When I look at my grandmother, I wonder whether any part of her remembers me. Any part that might still be tied to long-lost games of Snakes and Ladders, storytelling and holy communion. When I look at my grandmother, I wonder whether she has an answer for the time between waiting for school buses and waiting for me; the only daughter of her only daughter who left one day and just never came home.

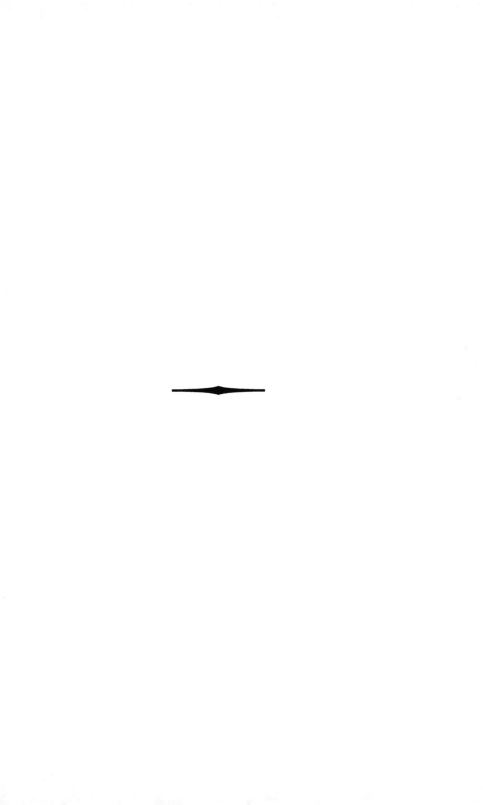

WALLS

MY LOVER IS a wall.

A stone wall.
A brick wall.
A high, mighty, sturdy wall.
A wall I am trying to climb, to conquer, to scale
without falling.

A wall so vast you can see it from the moon.

6513 miles of wall. 51 degrees high. 99 degrees wide. I listen
to her voice through oceans of fortress and phone line. I listen
to her voice through cracks in the stone.

But the wall is not just distance alone: The wall is her skin.
The wall is her flesh. The wall is the cage of her ribs that play
cavern to her leaky heart.

This heart that she has taken back to her kingdom on the
other side of the receiver.

Her elusive heart. Her traitorous heart. The heart for
which I will plunge my fists through delicately layered com-
binations of cement and tissue. The heart for which I will
charge through boundaries of bone and brick, make myself tall
like a giant, strong as lead, sure-footed as a cat with nothing
to lose.

My lover is a wall.

My lover of longitude, lover of latitude, lover of meeting points made up by coordinates. Can you hear me from over there? I am back-stepping. Getting ready to run. I am gaining speed, rushing up against your fort, defying gravity, scaling your skin.

I will find you on the other side.

———

Rome. 575 BC. King Servius sips on wine while demanding his workers build walls high enough to ensure that no enemy can invade the nucleus that is his territory.

His workers build the longest set of ancient walls still in a reasonable condition today. Canals were dug around the external perimeter to make them higher from the outside, mounds built on the internal circumference so that soldiers could keep watch from the inside.

To wall in.
To wall out.
To protect with.
To protect from.

A wall may be a single plane but it is characterised by its duality. It defines a space by dividing it. It brings together but keeps apart. It is passive offense but active defense.

It's me squinting at myself in a two-way mirror and hoping that you're looking back.

What the king did not know was that what would eventually cause his walls to give way was not some army with their cannons. Not some brave soldier with a human catapult. Not even divine intervention.

What would eventually crumble his walls was time. Time eating into stones with its insistent teeth. The wind-affirming impermanence with its constant seduction. The sun chasing ancient insects into cracks, rock coercing them into fossils. Time wearing away his fortress in the only way that time exhibits its linearity. Walls resist. Time insists.

Both persist.

But the wall still crumbles.

———————

I, too, have walls.

Walls the shape of my rotund silhouette.

Walls the curve of my welcoming smile.

Walls running the length of one arm to the other, as I reassure those who take shelter in my mass.

Because yes, I am massive. All curves and no edge, round like the globe. Round-eyed, round-lipped, circle upon circle. A spherical fortress with the strength of a planet.

Stoic. Undemanding. An excellent listener. Easy to talk to. Easier to cry to. They come to me, sit up against me, pour their hearts into my stone. Their secrets age under my weight like wine.

Because everybody needs someone to lean on.

Because everybody needs someone strong.

I acquire an army by doing nothing. They stand outside, never being let in.

Not all walls are solid.

When a forest fire is set alight, there are two sides to its face. On the safer side, fuel has already burnt; it is away from this side that fire travels.

In order to fight the flames effectively, one must stand on the *opposite* side; the direction in which the fire moves in search of more fuel. The fire must be faced head-on with the belief that one's body won't become the next thing it destroys. When doing this, sometimes, the fire retreats because it is diminishing; other times it retreats in order to expand around you.

Once it does this, you are encircled, enclosed within a wall of fire.

At this point, all the best smokejumpers know that the only way to escape is to run through the flames. It is this or death. They're equipped with special gear. They're equipped with years of training. They're equipped with the knowledge, the know-how, the consequences, and the back-up plans.

But when faced with a fire so high it blocks out the sky, so hot that it is licking the skin off your face, how does one unlearn everything already embedded in the gut? How does one run into the fire instead of running away? What eventually triggers that relinquishing of logic to faith, giving way to footsteps that run at the speed of one's pulse?

Are you really going to leave me like this? You, who struck a match up against my wooden heart and walked away?

Call to me, lover, from the other side. From beyond the crackling of flames and phone line. From outside the heat of this desire. Call to me louder than the screaming of trees. Than animals scattering and homeless. Than the flapping of wings and squawks of terror, as birds flee their nests, leaving behind only cracked eggs.

Call to me, lover, because if not with you, then for you, I burn.

They were disappointed, the Chinese, and so were we: The Great Wall couldn't actually be seen from the moon.

It had actually been a river, not a wall. Nature's, not ours. It should have been expected.

So disappointed were we that we blocked it out from our memories. The god-awful truth of our humanity: No single man-made structure is visible from such distance. We are tiny, insignificant, incapable of greatness.

Ironic, really, that despite our ingenuity, our ability to breathe without oxygen, trample space without weight, fly without wings, Nature still finds ways to outwit us: the speed of light, the limits of sight.

When you left, I believed that distance was an abstract concept. But it isn't. It is as tangible as the echo in my empty house. And I am disappearing, just like you wanted. Floating like a balloon into the sky.

But as my body ascends and breaks free from gravity, I watch you get smaller, and like all other details, the walls dissolve from sight.

———

My lover is the stone that walls me out.

My lover is the fire that walls me in.

My lover is a fortress so high and so wide, people have reported seeing her from the moon.

She will not respond to threats. She will not succumb to tears. She is not convinced by memory nor history and will not give in to fear.

But I've got time on my hands and poetry on my tongue. My hands the span of an ocean, my tongue as honest as brick.

I insist.
She resists.
I insist.
She resists.

I insist.
Again.
And again.

———

No one in Jericho expected it to happen. The rumbling sound that grew from a tiny but insistent vibration that seemed to come from the earth itself. That caused the muscles in everyone's calves to tremble just before it shot up through the foundation of the fortress, causing it to explode, matter spreading its fingers in every direction.

No one expected it, the minute Joshua gave the signal for the final war cry, the stones put together by hands of servants loyal and oppressed dislodging themselves from each other's grips, shattering in mid-air, defying every belief anyone might have had about gravity, physics, logic, God.

A wall is a very logical thing. It is there to divide. It is there to defend. It is there to protect. To climb a wall defies logic.

But must we be divided from each other? Protected from each other? Defended from each other?

People who believe in love have no concept of logic. Believing in anything immaterial requires faith, and logic has none. Logic requires proof, demands evidence, insists on facts. Joshua did not believe in logic. His army, most of whom thought he was crazy to be marching randomly around a city fortress, knew that too. However, no one argued.

Because military logic dictates that it is pointless to argue with an illogical man.

But on that seventh round, on that seventh day, as the priests, half-faithful, placed their lips to their mouthpieces, the war cry was followed by the deafening roar of logic collapsing in on itself.

The sound of walls exploding, caving, crumbling from what was no more than abstract instructions adhered to by a madman, caused everyone on both sides to fall to their knees, cover their ears, and pray.

————————

My lover is a wall. The perimeter of a civilisation 11 thousand years old. And within her, my city of springs giving swell to orchards of lemons. My city of palm trees that grow in the direction of the sun. My beloved city without whom I am homeless.

I will march around your kingdom seven times. One for each hour that keeps us apart. Because love commands that I do so and because I've never been one for logic.

Can you hear me, lover? Stretch seven days as long as you might. Create a world in which there is light. Cause oceans to distend, beseech trees to grow, throw birds into the air. On the sixth day, pluck a rib from the fortress of your heart and fashion a body you believe you can love.

Because on the seventh day, when you put your feet up on the couch, forgetting about a time when only chaos existed, that is when I will come for you; jump into your kingdom straight from the moon, draw you home like the tides, plummet back into your heart with gravity the weight of bricks.

Wait for me, lover. For my binocular arms. For my eyes like fire. For my marching footfalls attuned to your pulse. Because with time and tongue, I insist, again.

And the walls come crumbling down.

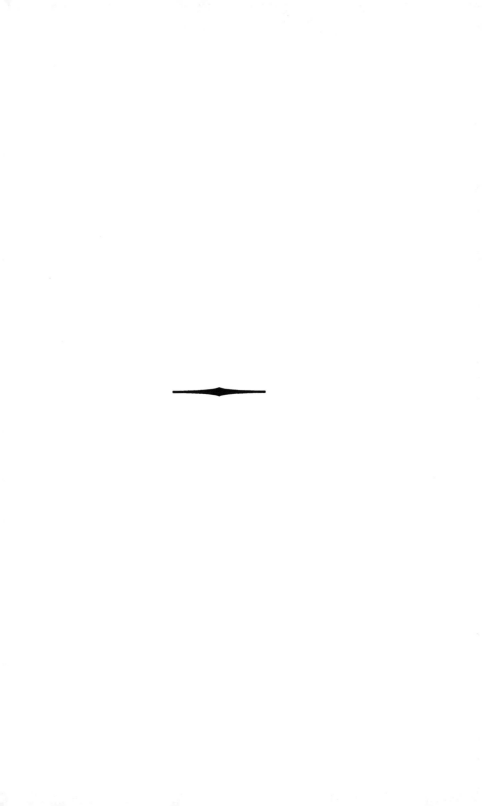

FROM THE GROUND UP

BLUEPRINTS

DURING MY FREQUENT house-moving, I came to understand how this city has no patience for those who cannot, or do not wish to, acclimatise to change. You like old neighbourhoods, unrenovated housing, nature growing wild? Good luck. You want to live a simple life outside of cheques and balances? Just try. Technology will urge itself into your pockets. Highways will encroach upon your gardens. Luxury housing will impress itself upon your land and upon the cemeteries of your ancestors. Prices will skyrocket out of your control and if you're not working, always working, urge you back into your parents' homes, or out into the streets.

When public housing grew to be the nation's highest priority, the need to fit everyone into state-sanctioned boxes became a task of the highest order. No more of these zinc-roofed monstrosities parading as households. Not to mention those attap-walled nooks hanging off the edges of shorelines. How to maintain security when you could pick the padlock on any one of these doors and barge your way into someone else's life?

We needed to be organised. Separated. Resettled. Squatting was a sure sign of trouble. So we built. And we built. And we never quite stopped. By the 60s, one in ten lived in public housing. By the mid-80s, eight in ten. The government had done it. Housing for the masses. When we ran out of land, we stole it from the sea. And once we ran out of that, we tore it down again so that we could start over. Put the people in their flats, the leaders said. All that is wild must be contained.

Even nature must be boxed. Mow down fruit orchards for shopping centres. Uproot trees and replant them in straight lines. Then cut those down in order to build better ones. Make them out of steel so you won't need to water them! Let them be bulletproof, windproof, human-proof, nature-proof—the tourist attraction of the century! Robot trees for our robot people. The billion dollars will go a long way. Meanwhile, as flash floods assault small pockets of urbanity, a tree pushes itself out of the narrow strip of soil that flanks my house. A year ago, this tree did not exist. Today, it grows taller than our roof. My landlord keeps pressing me to cut it down.

I refuse.

———————

Once the 80s were upon us, we embraced capitalism with a sort of fervor which has not diminished in the last 30 years of nation-building. We wanted all the privileges of Western opulence without compromising "Asian Values." We invited the world into our shopping malls and into our homes. By the 90s, we'd bought into the dream. We wanted all the key words: *bigger, better, faster, richer, leaner, cleaner.*

Cleaner. We'd wanted *cleaner* right from the very beginning. We were told that turning hand-built homes into high-rise housing was about rescuing ourselves from slums: Look at how unhygienic those people were, drawing bathwater from wells. How unruly their lines of laundry at the mercy of the wind. How distasteful their children playing in the mud. Wipe it all out in one fell swoop. We'll pave over their nudity with brick walls. We'll elevate them out of sight. We'll manufacture a dream, a city of the future. Their children will live safe and out of grasp, closer to the sky than to the sand. They will thank us one day, when they are rich, when their bare feet never have to touch the soil.

Singapore's obsession with cleanliness is a lot like Lady Macbeth's repeated washing of her hands: memories of the crimes we committed in the name of progress, caked underneath our fingernails. Because even when the streets sparkle with the sweat of underpaid cleaners, even when our galleries glisten with the impotence of regulated art, even when our sterile hearts are dubbed the least emotional in the world, still we obsess ourselves with the eradication of mess: Out, out damn spot!

———————

"I could not face those rough women," he laughed, not detecting the look of discomfort in the journalist's eyes.

Her smile wavered, but only for a moment. Her straight face had come with years of practice. And the man would probably not have been able to detect it anyway. He was too flattered that the newspapers wanted to dedicate an entire spread to him to notice anything except his own joy that day. He could not stop talking. He was sure he was nailing it.

"They were cursing and swearing. I ran up to my office through the back door, you know?" He burst into a huge guffaw. He made sure to highlight again the fact that they were women, and spoke about how he had never forgotten how bad they smelled. Pig farmers, they were. The thought of them banging at his door made him laugh all over again.

He remembered wishing that the people knew what was good for them. He, of course, did not mean this in a patronising way. He truly wanted what was best for the people. He was, after all, doing this job for free. What better demonstration of his intentions could he provide? Besides, how long could the local population live in these slums, with light provided by makeshift lamps? How long could chickens and pigs be reared as financial investments? The rest of the world was moving along and we were being left behind. The country needed to be cleaned up.

Build houses.

That was the brief given. He admired how succinct the command had been. How something as complex as this housing problem, as difficult as this upcoming task, could be summed up in two simple words. A verb, a noun: *Build. Houses.*

He knew what he had to do. The nation was depending on him. People needed homes. Everyone was living in unruly communities from which crime sprung too regularly. Such sorrow he felt for the poor and such fear he felt for the country's well-being, that under his watch, he built in two years what his predecessors had built in over 30. He was a wizard divining a problem and solving it.

He was unstoppable. By the time the city started becoming a reality, he was in complete control. What he said, went. What he disliked, disappeared. When he asked that a building be torn down because it appeared slanted, it was torn down.

In that same vein, squatters were evicted from their premises and moved into new flats. Rent, which had previously comprised the price of Storm King gas lamps and common water pipes, was now often unaffordable. Rearing poultry to help with income was no longer allowed. Many found themselves moving back to the slums. Some found themselves at door in protest, like those women who had smelled worse than the pigs they reared. He looked at the reporter once again, reminding her of how he had done everything out of the goodness of his heart, that he had not taken a single cent for the his first three years in which nation-building had become his job. *Can you imagine how* . . .

"Did you feel bad, though?" she interjected, finally unable to contain herself. Awkward silence and raised eyebrows. He had no idea what she was talking about. She worried that she would not be able to properly contain the irritation that seemed to be creeping into every part of her face.

"I mean, for the squatters. Did you feel bad forcing them out of their homes?" Silence. What was this girl babbling about? He was the one who'd *built* their homes. What kind of country would we be living in if we'd chosen to remain in our own squalor?

So long as they were out of sight, they were out of mind. These dark-skinned foreigners so lucky to have found work in our country. And even luckier to have been housed in the centre of a good neighbourhood, surrounded by such vulnerable families. When the dormitory was finally built, the entrance was located at the opposite end of the estate; no need to worry about our wives and sisters. No need to worry about our pin-afored daughters who make their way to school and back. If anything, they would stare at the girls through the steel fences. Two million dollars was spent making sure that the workers could be driven straight from the highways to the dormitory; a slip road that would ensure that no one who did not want to see these dirty men would ever have to.

When Bhavan passed the newly built dorm, he wondered what the inside of it looked like. He remembered his brother Ashutosh saying that residents were unhappy about the idea of the dormitory being constructed. They said it would make the area dangerous and smelly. From outside, it looked spacious. Spacious enough for community, for time spent sitting in the open spaces after work. He wondered whether the company would end up moving in. But he knew that what was seen on the outside might not necessarily be reflected on the inside. He wondered how Ashutosh was doing. He had not seen him for three weeks as he had decided to spend the last three Sundays doing some overtime work for the boss. He was low on funds and wanted to send his son some extra money for his birthday.

When he first landed, Bhavan had been full of hope. He had heard many things about Singapore—clean streets, fair government, lots of opportunity. His cousin had a friend who had gone to work in the construction industry and had come back a wealthy man. Another who had worked in the studio of a ceramicist and had come back knowing how to make pots. The possibilities were endless. As for Bhavan, he would be helping to build a luxury condominium in the centre of the town. He had held back tears at the airport as he waved goodbye to Asya and picked Balaraj up, telling him to take care of his mother. But he had been excited at the prospect of working so close to the heart of the city. Happy with the idea that he would now be able to take good care of his family.

When he first arrived at his dorm, a small swell of disappointment welled up inside him. He wondered why he was being taken directly to a worksite instead of his place of lodging. A Chinese man in a hard hat looked at him and the other workers who'd come with him and snorted something in dialect to his colleague. They laughed, as the foreman directed the workers to the rooms that had been built up beneath the construction site, where they would be staying. When Bhavan turned the stair, he saw rows of double-decker beds, lined side by side, stretching to the end of the long basement.

"Ah. Here got friend many many. That one bed, you taking."

Lucky, he thought, that he had not brought much with him. There was barely any walking space between the beds and no storage space at all. The men strung raffia from bed to bed, hanging their washed clothes up. The laundry also allowed them some semi-privacy from one another. But he would soon learn that his coworkers preferred to take them down at night, even if they weren't dry. The hanging clothes impaired what little circulation there was in this room where there were no fans, minimal draft, and barely any natural light.

The smell of wet clothes kept indoors too long assaulted his nostrils. As he approached the end of the room, the smell of curry sitting too long upon the stove hit him as well. Around the corner, two squatting toilets, one of which was not working, three hosepipes, and a bench. For a moment, he thought of his Asya, and of Balaraj, and wondered whether he had made a mistake. He shook off the thought. Even if he wanted to go back, he wouldn't be able to. He needed to pay off the middleman who had brought him here and would have to work at least a year to do that. If he went back now, his family would starve. This would have to be home for the next two years. He would work hard and he would work well. He would leave this place a better man with a better life.

Bhavan thought back to those days as he made his way past the Serangoon Gardens dormitory. He thought about the things he had hoped for before landing in Singapore, and the things he had since gotten used to. Worried that something might have happened to Ashutosh, he decided to give him a call. When the attempt revealed only a dial tone, he sat on the hard concrete by the fencing, overwhelmed by sudden and unexpected sorrow. He placed his face in his hands and sat like that for a while.

A woman walked by, holding hands with a child who pinched her nose shut as they passed him.

The day we were put into flats, we consented to being controlled. Only certain families were allowed to purchase "public" housing. Communities were disrupted and disempowered. Women and men fell victim to households that relegated women to childcare and men to breadwinning. The multifamily networks in which children were once raised were broken up and could now be micromanaged. By the end of the 1980s, all HDB tenants were subjected to free publications that taught them how to be modern city-dwellers. Tips included features of selected flats that were thought to be well-designed, just in case you wanted to emulate your superior neighbours. It included gentle reminders that decorating your house using a non-approved contractor would result in hefty fines, that keeping a cat in your home would incur the same result, that investing in domestic consumption was the same as investing in emotional attachment. *Our Home*, it was called. As if we could not remember where we were. Not *my* home, not *your* home, and certainly not *theirs*. Remember, this is our home, and this is how you must act. Here are things to cook. This is how you adapt. Here, look at our cover pictures. These are the sorts of families you should have. Look at these smiling children. Don't you want this? Who doesn't want this? You must want this. We should want this.

I want to live in a house with roots. Roots buried deep into the ground. It will be a living house, a breathing house, a house made of brick and bone. It will not crumble under the weight of one's hand. It will not shift with the wind or dissolve in the rain. It will be filled with laughter and music and sunlight and flowers and books and art and sex.

But I am afraid that this is the cycle we are doomed to repeat: low-rise will become high-rise, cemeteries will become train stations, libraries will become gaping holes, and the new will never get a chance to grow old. The only thing that will age in this land is us. Alienation is inevitable; a destiny to be proud of, to be embraced.

Don't get me wrong. We are not an unhappy people. Unhappy people are people who do not get what they need. We cannot be unhappy because we don't know what we need. We don't know what we need because we don't know who we are. We don't know who we are because we don't remember who we were. We've lost all reference points. We've burnt our photo albums. We face forward, walk in straight lines, never looking back.

I look at my students, and they are happy to live without memory. They leave their remembering to machines. The only thing they care to keep in mind is which machine they saved what on. Families are phone numbers. Friends are photos. Childhoods are cyberlands held between palms on buses, trains, and Saturday nights out. I ask them what they think about culture and they tell me that culture is a temple no longer relevant to them, and that their grandparents must have led boring lives because they didn't have the Internet.

I want history. Is that too romantic for us children of the future? Too abstract? Does it not have enough fixed dimensions for our geometrical minds? For our boxes that used to be hearts?

And I don't want the sort of history that is linear. I don't want timelines running parallel to each other, divided by markers and labeled with dates. I don't want the kind of history taught for the purpose of propaganda and patriotism; the kind of past created to secure a safe future.

I want *history*. The moss that grows on walls, wounds that scar the skin, wrong turns, cracks in the stone, archaeologies of desire dug up like dirty laundry and flapping like wings in every backyard.

I want to remember the name of the street on which I was born, before it is gone. Before I am gone.

I want live in a house with roots. I want to remember.

HOME

DESPITE SCIENTIFIC DISCOVERIES, there are still people who believe that the rock pigeon's ability to return to its original point of origin for a distance of up to two thousand kilometres is related to an inborn connection between a bird and its mate. I've heard that king penguins have a similar connection to their young. If you were to camouflage yourself in a flock of 600,000 penguins across the ice-white coast of Tierra del Fuego, you would most likely be unable to differentiate one bird from the other. When a parent goes off looking for food, brown fuzzy chicks run all over the place, perfectly indistinguishable, a mass of chaos. But when the parent returns from the hunt, belly full of fresh squid, all they have to do is call. The parent squawks and the chick whistles. The pair spend hours wading through lines of tuxedo jackets till the two are finally reunited.

Perhaps observations of nature are the reason we've spun strong conceptions of love and family impossible to follow through on into tales that govern our lives. Some radar that leaves us always either searching or settling for what we believe we long for. Something burned into parts of our brains; into the parts of our hearts that still wish to belong.

Even termites, after all, listen to an inner call when they take flight, heading, doubtless, to the moon. The biological purpose of this is to take them as far from their original colony as possible, so as to spread the species as far as it can unfold. No termite, of course, ever reaches the moon. It is just a source of light that approximates a distance that can never be reached. In worlds where concrete takes up more space than land, they fly, instead, towards our street lamps and into our houses, trailing, wingless, after the light that leaks from our windows.

I suspect that many of us still want to believe in love. A love that goes beyond the biological urges that possess our bodies and beyond the chemicals that feed our fairy tales. If biology is destiny, then perhaps the body was made to desire love despite the destruction that it brings. But even so, that desire gets diluted into 50-thousand-dollar weddings, bad television dramas, and tiresome rituals we have come to embrace. It becomes a love that is more digestible, less frightening, easier to stand by. Sometimes we dilute it into a God for whom we burn with passion or the children we burden with passion lost. Either way, we call it love because we want to believe that there is a force larger than us that makes us capable of caring about something more than ourselves. A force untouched by the exterior world. The closest thing we have to permanence. The closest thing we have to home. Physical geography is a barrier that can be conquered with an aeroplane or with bird-like instinct. Interior geography is an ocean so vast, that to love must be to walk on water. And we want to believe we are capable of miracles.

The movers arrive at my new apartment as I close the door on this chapter. And just as this story started with you, so it shall end. May it cut through kilometres to find you. May it shelter you from the rain. May it find you nestled at the end of my voice.

I have grown so used to raised rents and evictions that I disguise my moving boxes as furniture. This way, if I am forced to leave in a hurry, I am packed before I even have to go. Look at them, propping up desks and nightstands, disguised in blankets and shawls. If the next place I find cannot accommodate my belongings, I learn to do without them. When the need for basic shelter eventually takes over the attachment of meanings to objects, sentiment is the first to go. No longer can one attach memories to monuments, or affection to architecture. Emptying the house cannot involve emptying the heart when one has to do it so often.

At some point, the evictions seeped into my chest and I started treating friends like houses. I leave when the walls fall apart, when the roof gets leaky, when the structure becomes unsound. Gone, without a word. I stow grudges away in mental boxes and once the space has run out, I find new places to go. It is hard, after disowning your own parents, not to disown every person whose love does not meet your standards. When you've survived the former, you understand that you will also survive the latter.

Walking out of my mother's house, I felt cowardly but was called brave. Neither of these is completely true. For the most part, what I was, was desperate. The further I grow away from her, the harder it is to deny that leaving was not just about the trauma of what had happened, but also the trauma of what would. I did not need to be thrown out of the house to understand that I was being rejected. And I wanted to reject her before she got a chance to reject me. If I don't belong to my mother, to whom do I belong?

Notions of family are so fragile, everyone wants to own them. Religion. Culture. Conservatives. Liberals. No matter which camp is talking about it, family becomes the moral microcosm of what constitutes a good life.

I grew up not understanding how family was supposed to feel. It was only when you left, that I realised what I'd been missing for so many years. You'd filled a space I had not even known was empty and by the time I realised this, the space was empty again.

Is this karma? Me leaving my family and then having my family leave me?

Coming home to someone is many things. It is a literal action, an abstract idea, a physical feeling. It is more than the sound of the key turning in the door and the voice that calls from the porch. It is a choice, a promise, a declaration. It is a return, not as a person to a place, but as oneself to another. It is one person saying to another person: *You are the one I choose.*

I don't know how to tell you this, after all this time. That you are family. That it is to you I wish to return. That my house is not a home, and that without you, waking up any-where means being in the wrong place.

Boxes are being offloaded from the truck. Objects are being moved into a new apartment. The refrigerator is being plugged in, shelves reassembled. That old smell of new paint. A sigh of relief.

The first thing I unpack is the typewriter you bought, six years and seven apartments ago. I place it on the desk and think of how we once stood, you on one side of the gate, me on the other.

Come home to me, lover. The door is open. The bed is made. Of my flesh, make a dwelling, to my voice, fall asleep.

Open the door. Break down the walls. Take off your shoes. Choose *me*.

ACKNOWLEDGMENTS

The chapter titled "Walls" was originally published as "My Jericho" in *GASPP: A Gay Anthology of Singapore Poetry & Prose* (The Literary Centre, 2010).

Tania De Rozario would like to thank the following:

Jee Leong Koh and the Gaudy Boy team—for bringing this book to North America. Kenny Leck and the Math Paper Press team—for its initial publication in 2016. Cyril Wong—for your words, which I revisit again and again. Lynn Lu—for your art, which I revisit again and again. My chosen family—Robin, Corinna, Dana, Lisa, Koki, Jane. My forever sisters—Michaela and Jackie. My partner—The Verniest of all Verns.

ABOUT THE AUTHOR

Tania De Rozario is a writer and visual artist. She is the author of *Tender Delirium* (2013) and *Somewhere Else, Another You* (2018), published by Math Paper Press. *And the Walls Come Crumbling Down* (2016) was first published in Singapore by Math Paper Press before the 2020 North American Gaudy Boy edition.

Her work has been published in journals and anthologies, including *The Malahat Review*, *Sow's Ear Poetry Review*, *Prairie Schooner Online Journal*, *Blue Lyra Review*, *The Margins*, *carte blanche*, *SOFTBLOW*, and *Punch Drunk Press*. Her visual art has been showcased in galleries and art spaces in Singapore, Moscow, Amsterdam, London, Spain, and San Francisco. She has written extensively about art for both institutional and commercial publications, with a focus on art from Singapore and Southeast Asia.

For 12 years, Tania worked as an adjunct at LASALLE College of the Arts, where she taught a variety of classes across the McNally School of Fine Arts and the Faculty for the Creative Industries. Her most recent work there involved creating and facilitating a 12-week lecture/workshop that focused on Feminine Monstrosities in Contemporary Cinema. She was also the director and co-founder of EtiquetteSG, a platform that developed and showcased art, writing, and film by women from and in Singapore. Founded in 2010, its most recent work included the development and facilitation of art and writing workshops focused on issues of gender-based violence.

ABOUT GAUDY BOY

From the Latin *gaudium*, meaning "joy," Gaudy Boy publishes books that delight readers with the various powers of art. The name is taken from the poem "Gaudy Turnout," by Singaporean poet Arthur Yap, about his time abroad in Leeds, the United Kingdom. Similarly inspired by such diasporic wanderings and migrations, Gaudy Boy brings literary works by authors of Asian heritage to the attention of an American audience and beyond. Established in 2018 as the imprint of the New York City-based literary nonprofit Singapore Unbound, we publish poetry, fiction, and literary nonfiction. Visit our website at www.singaporeunbound.org/gaudyboy.

WINNERS OF THE GAUDY BOY POETRY BOOK PRIZE
Play for Time by Paula Mendoza
Autobiography of Horse by Jenifer Sang Eun Park
The Experiment of the Tropics by Lawrence Lacambra Ypil

FICTION
The Foley Artist by Ricco Villanueva Siasoco
Malay Sketches by Alfian Sa'at